A

DISCOURSE

OCCASIONED BY THE

DEATH OF DANIEL WEBSTER,

PREACHED AT THE MELODEON

ON SUNDAY, OCTOBER 31, 1852.

BY

THEODORE PARKER,

MINISTER OF THE TWENTY-EIGHTH CONGREGATIONAL SOCIETY IN BOSTON.

BOSTON:

BENJAMIN B. MUSSEY & CO.

No. 29, Cornhill.

1853.

BOSTON:
PRINTED BY JOHN WILSON AND SON, SCHOOL STREET.

PREFACE.

It is now four months since the delivery of this Sermon. A phonographic report of it was published the next morning, and quite extensively circulated in all parts of the country. Since then, I have taken pains to examine anew the life and actions of the distinguished man who is the theme of the discourse. I have carefully read all the criticisms on my estimate of him, which came to hand; I have diligently read the most important sermons and other discourses which treat of him, and have conversed with persons who have known Mr. Webster at all the various periods of his life. The result is embodied in the following pages.

My estimate of Mr. Webster differs from that which seems to prevail just now in Church and State; differs widely, differs profoundly. I did not suppose that my judgment upon him would pass unchallenged. I have not been surprised at the swift condemnation which many men have pronounced upon this sermon, — upon the statements therein, and the motives thereto. I should be sorry to find that Americans valued a great man so little as to have nothing to say in defence of one so long and so conspicuously before the public. The violence and rage directed against me is not astonishing; it is not even new. I am not vain enough to fancy that I have never been mistaken in a fact of Mr. Webster's history, or in my judgment pronounced on any of his actions, words, or motives. I can only say I have done what I could.

If I have committed any errors, I hope they will be pointed out. Fifty years hence, the character of Mr. Webster and his eminent contemporaries will be better understood than now; for we have not yet all the evidence on which the final judgment of posterity will rest. Thomas Hutchinson and John Adams are better known now than at the day of their death; five and twenty years hence they will both be better known than at present.

BOSTON, March 7, 1853.

INTRODUCTION.

TO THE YOUNG MEN OF AMERICA.

GENTLEMEN, — I address this Discourse to you in particular, and by way of introduction will say a few words.

We are a young nation, three and twenty millions strong, rapidly extending in our geographic spread, enlarging rapidly in numerical power, and greatening our material strength with a swiftness which has no example. Soon we shall spread over the whole continent, and number a hundred million men. America and England are but parts of the same nation, — a younger and an older branch of the same great Anglo-Saxon stem. Our character will affect that of the mother-country, as her good and evil still influence us. Considering the important place which the Anglo-Saxon tribe holds in the world at this day, — occupying one-eighth part of the earth, and controlling one-sixth part of its inhabitants, — the national character of England and America becomes one of the great human forces which is to control the world for some ages to come.

In the American character there are some commanding and noble qualities. We have founded some political and ecclesiastical institutions which seem to me the proudest achievements of mankind in Church and State. But there are other qualities in the nation's character which are mean and selfish; we have founded other institutions, or confirmed such as we inherited, which were the weakness of a former and darker age, and are the shame of this.

The question comes, Which qualities shall prevail in the character and in the institutions of America, — the noble, or the mean and selfish? Shall America govern herself by the eternal laws, as they are discerned through the conscience of mankind, or by the transient appetite of the hour, — the lust for land, for money, for power, or fame? That is a question for you to settle; and, as you decide for God or mammon, so follows the weal or woe of millions of men. Our best institutions are an experiment: shall it fail? If so, it will be through your fault. You have the power to make it succeed. We have nothing to fear from any foreign foe, much to dread from Wrong at home: will you suffer that to work our overthrow?

The two chief forms of American action are Business and Politics, — the commercial and the political form. The two humbler forms of our activity, the Church and the Press, — the ecclesiastic and the literary form, — are subservient to the others. Hence it becomes exceedingly important to study carefully our commercial and political action, criticizing both by the Absolute Right; for they control the development of the people, and determine our character. The commercial and political forces of the time culminate in the leading politicians, who represent those forces in their persons, and direct the energies of the people to evil or to good.

It is for this reason, young men, that I have spoken so many times from the pulpit on the great political questions of the day, and on the great political men; for this reason did I preach, and now again publish, this Discourse on one of the most eminent Americans of our day, — that men may be warned of the evil in our Business and our State, and be guided to the Eternal Justice which is the foundation of the common weal. There is a Higher Law of God, written imperishably on the nature of things, and in the nature of man; and, if this nation continually violates that law, then we fall a ruin to the ground.

If there be any truth, any justice, in my counsel, I hope you will be guided thereby; and, in your commerce and politics, will practise on the truth which ages confirm, that Righteousness exalteth a Nation, while Injustice is a reproach to any People.

DISCOURSE.

When Bossuet, who was himself the eagle of eloquence, preached the funeral discourse on Henrietta Maria, daughter of Henry the Fourth of France, and wife of Charles the First of England, he had a task far easier than mine to-day. She was indeed the queen of misfortunes; the daughter of a king assassinated in his own capital, and the widow of a king judicially put to death in front of his own palace. Her married life was bounded by the murder of her royal sire, and the execution of her kingly spouse; and she died neglected, far from kith and kin. But for that great man, who in his youth was called, prophetically, a "Father of the Church," the sorrows of her birth and her estate made it easy to gather up the audience in his arms, to moisten the faces of men with tears, to show them the nothingness of mortal glory, and the beauty of eternal life. He led his hearers to his conclusion that day, as the mother lays the sobbing child to her bosom to still its grief.

To-day it is not so with me. Of all my public trials, this is my most trying day. Give me your sympathies, my friends; remember the difficulty of my position,—its delicacy too.

2

I am to speak of one of the most conspicuous men that New England ever bore, — conspicuous, not by accident, but by the nature of his mind, — one of her ablest intellects. I am to speak of an eminent man, of great power, in a great office, one of the landmarks of politics, now laid low. He seemed so great that some men thought he was himself one of the institutions of America. I am to speak while his departure is yet but of yesterday; while the sombre flags still float in our streets. I am no party man; you know I am not. No party is responsible for me, nor I to any one. I am free to commend the good things of all parties, — their great and good men; free likewise to censure the evil of all parties. You will not ask me to say what only suits the public ear: there are a hundred to do that to-day. I do not follow opinion because popular. I cannot praise a man because he had great gifts, great station, and great opportunities; I cannot harshly censure a man for trivial mistakes. You will not ask me to flatter because others flatter; to condemn because the ruts of condemnation are so deep and so easy to travel in. It is unjust to be ungenerous, either in praise or blame: only the truth is beautiful in speech. It is not reverential to treat a great man like a spoiled child. Most of you are old enough to know that good and evil are both to be expected of each man. I hope you are all wise enough to discriminate between right and wrong.

Give me your sympathies. This I am sure of, — I shall be as tender in my judgment as a woman's love; I will try to be as fair as the justice of a man. I shall tax your time beyond even my usual wont, for I cannot crush Olympus into a nut. Be not alarmed: if I tax your time the more, I shall tire your patience less. Such a day as this will never come again to you or me. There is no DANIEL WEBSTER left to die, and Nature will not soon give us another such as he. I will take care by my speech that you sit easy on your bench. The theme will take care that you remember what I say.

A great man is the blossom of the world; the individual and prophetic flower, parent of seeds that will be men. This is the greatest work of God; far transcending earth and moon and sun, and all the material magnificence of the universe. It is "a little lower than the angels," and, like the aloe-tree, it blooms but once an age. So we should value, love, and cherish it the more. America has not many great men living now, — scarce one: there have been few in her history. Fertile in multitudes, she is stingy in great men, — her works mainly achieved by large bodies of but common men. At this day, the world has not many natural masters. There is a dearth of great men. England is no better off than we her child. Sir Robert Peel has for years been dead. Wellington's soul has gone home, and left his body awaiting burial. In France, Germany, Italy, and Russia, few great men appear. The Revolution of 1848, which found every thing else, failed because it found not them. A sad Hungarian weeps over the hidden crown of Maria Theresa; and a sadder countenance drops a tear for the nation of Dante, and the soil of Virgil and Cæsar, Lucretius and Cicero. To me these two seem the greatest men of Europe now. There are great chemists, great geologists, great philologians; but of great men, Christendom has not many. From the highest places of politics great men recede, and in all Europe no kingly intellect now throbs beneath a royal crown. Even Nicholas of Russia is only tall, not great.

But here let us pause a moment, and see what greatness is, looking at the progressive formation of the idea of a great man. In general, greatness is eminence of ability; so there are as many different forms thereof as there are qualities wherein a man may be eminent. These various forms of greatness should be distinctly marked, that, when we say a man is great, we may know exactly what we mean.

In the rudest ages, when the body is man's only tool for work or war, eminent strength of body is the thing most coveted. Then, and so long as human affairs are controlled by brute force, the giant is thought to be the great man,— is had in honor for his eminent brute strength.

When men have a little outgrown that period of force, cunning is the quality most prized. The nimble brain outwits the heavy arm, and brings the circumvented giant to the ground. He who can overreach his antagonist, plotting more subtly, winning with more deceitful skill; who can turn and double on his unseen track, "can smile and smile, and be a villain,"— he is the great man.

Brute force is merely animal; cunning is the animalism of the intellect,— the mind's least intellectual element. As men go on in their development, finding qualities more valuable than the strength of the lion or the subtlety of the fox, they come to value higher intellectual faculties,— great understanding, great imagination, great reason. Power to think is then the faculty men value most; ability to devise means for attaining ends desired; the power to originate ideas, to express them in speech, to organize them into institutions; to organize things into a machine, men into an army, or a state, or a gang of operatives; to administer these various organizations. He who is eminent in this ability is thought the great man.

But there are qualities nobler than the mere intellect, the moral, the affectional, the religious faculties,— the power of justice, of love, of holiness, of trust in God, and of obedience to his law,— the Eternal Right. These are the highest qualities of man: whoso is most eminent therein is the greatest of great men. He is as much above the merely intellectual great men, as they above the men of mere cunning or of force.

Thus, then, we have four different kinds of greatness. Let me name them bodily greatness, crafty greatness, intellectual greatness, religious greatness. Men in different degrees of development will value the different kinds of greatness.

Belial cannot yet honor Christ. How can the little girl appreciate Aristotle and Kant? The child thinks as a child. You must have manhood in you to honor it in others, even to see it.

Yet how we love to honor men eminent in such modes of greatness as we can understand! Indeed, we must do so. Soon as we really see a real great man, his magnetism draws us, will we or no. Do any of you remember when, for the first time in adult years, you stood beside the ocean, or some great mountain of New Hampshire, or Virginia, or Pennsylvania, or the mighty mounts that rise in Switzerland? Do you remember what emotions came upon you at the awful presence? But if you were confronted by a man of vast genius, of colossal history and achievements, immense personal power of wisdom, justice, philanthropy, religion, of mighty power of will and mighty act; if you feel him as you feel the mountain and the sea, what grander emotions spring up! It is like making the acquaintance of one of the elementary forces of the earth, — like associating with gravitation itself! The stiffest neck bends over: down go the democratic knees; human nature is loyal then! A New England shipmaster, wrecked on an island in the Indian Sea, was seized by his conquerors, and made their chief. Their captive became their king. After years of rule, he managed to escape. When he once more visited his former realm, he found that the savages had carried him to heaven, and worshipped him as a god greater than their fancied deities: he had revolutionized divinity, and was himself enthroned as a god. Why so? In intellectual qualities, in religious qualities, he was superior to their idea of God, and so they worshipped him. So loyal is human nature to its great men.

Talk of Democracy! — we are all looking for a master; a man manlier than we. We are always looking for a great man to solve the difficulty too hard for us, to break the rock which lies in our way, — to represent the possibility of human nature as an ideal, and then to realize that ideal in his life. Little boys in the country, working against time, with stents to do, long for the passing-by of some tall brother, who in a few minutes shall achieve what the smaller boy took hours to do. And we are all of us but little boys, looking for some great brother to come and help us end our tasks.

But it is not quite so easy to recognize the greatest kind of greatness. A Nootka-Sound Indian would not see much in Leibnitz, Newton, Socrates, or Dante; and if a great man were to come as much before us as we are before the Nootka-Sounders, what should we say of him? Why, the worst names we could devise, — Infidel, Atheist, Blasphemer, Hypocrite. Perhaps we should dig up the old cross, and make a new martyr of the man posterity will worship as a deity. It is the men who are up that see the rising sun, not the sluggards. It takes greatness to see greatness, and know it at the first; I mean to see greatness of the highest kind. Bulk, anybody can see; bulk of body or mind. The loftiest form of greatness is never popular in its time. Men cannot understand or receive it. Guinea negroes would think a juggler a greater man than Franklin. What would be thought of Martin Luther at Rome, of Washington at St. Petersburg, of Fenelon among the Sacs and Foxes? Herod and Pilate were popular in their day, — men of property and standing. They got nominations and honor enough. Jesus of Nazareth got no nomination, got a cross between two thieves, was crowned with thorns, and, when he died, eleven Galileans gathered together to lament their Lord. Any man can measure a walking-stick, — so many hands long, and so many nails beside; but it takes a mountain-intellect to measure the Andes and Altai.

But, now and then, God creates a mighty man, who greatly influences mankind. Sometimes he reaches far on into other ages. Such a man, if he be of the greatest, will, by and by, unite in himself the four chief forces of society, — business, politics, literature, and the church. Himself a stronger force than all of these, he will at last control the commercial, political, literary, and ecclesiastical action of mankind. But just as he is greater than other men, in the highest mood of greatness, will he at first be opposed, and hated too. The tall house in the street darkens the grocer's window opposite, and he must strike his light sooner than before. The inferior great man does not understand the man of superior modes of eminence. Sullenly the full moon at morning pales her ineffectual light before the rising day. In the Greek fable, jealous Saturn devours the new gods whom he feared, foreseeing the day when the Olympian dynasty would turn him out of heaven. To the natural man the excellence of the spiritual is only foolishness. What do you suppose the best educated Pharisees in Jerusalem thought of Jesus? They thought him an infidel: "He blasphemeth." They called him crazy: "he hath a devil." They mocked at the daily beauty of his holiness: he had "broken the sabbath." They reviled at his philanthropy: it was "eating with publicans and sinners."

Human nature loves to reverence great men, and often honors many a little one under the mistake that he is great. See how nations honor the greatest great men, — Moses, Zoroaster, Socrates, Jesus — that loftiest of men! But by how many false men have we been deceived, — men whose light leads to bewilder, and dazzles to blind! If a preacher is a thousand years before you and me, we cannot understand him. If only a hundred years of thought shall separate us, there is a great gulf between the two, whereover neither Dives nor Abraham, nor yet Moses himself, can pass. It is a false great man often who gets possession of the pulpit, with his lesson for to-day, which is no lesson; and a false great man who gets a throne, with his lesson for to-day, which is also no lesson. Men great in little things are sure of their pay. It is all ready, subject to their order.

A little man is often mistaken for a great one. The possession of office, of accidental renown, of imposing qualities, of brilliant eloquence, often dazzles the beholder; and he reverences a show.

How much a great man of the highest kind can do for us, and how easy! It is not harder for a cloud to thunder, than for a chestnut in a farmer's fire to snap. Dull Mr. Jingle urges along his restive, hardmouthed donkey, besmouched with mire, and wealed with many a stripe, amid the laughter of the boys; while, by his proper motion, swan-like Milton flies before the faces of mankind, which are new lit with admiration at the poet's rising flight, his garlands and singing robes about him, till the aspiring glory transcends the sight, yet leaves its track of beauty trailed across the sky.

Intellect and conscience are conversant with ideas, — with absolute truth and absolute right, as the norm of conduct. But, with most men, the affections are developed in advance of the intellect and the conscience; and the affections want a person. In his actions, a man of great intellect embodies a principle, good or bad; and, by the affections, men accept the great intellectual man, bad or good, and with him the principle he has got.

As the affections are so large in us, how delightful is it for us to see a great man, honor him, love him, reverence him, trust him! Crowds of men come to look upon a hero's face, who are all careless of his actions and heedless of his thought; they know not his what, nor his whence, nor his whither; his person passes for reason, justice, and religion.

They say that women have the most of this affection, and so are most attachable, most swayed by persons, — least by ideas. Woman's mind and conscience, and her soul, they say, are easily crushed into her all-embracing heart; and truth, justice, and holiness are trodden under foot by her affection, rushing towards its object. "What folly!" say men. But, when a man of large intellect comes, he is wont to make women of us all, and take us by the heart. Each great intellectual man, if let alone, will have an influence in proportion to his strength of mind and will, — the good great man, the bad great man; for as each particle of matter has an attractive force, which affects all other matter, so each particle of mind has an attractive force, which draws all other mind.

How pleasant it is to love and reverence! To idle men how much more delightful is it than to criticize a man, take him to pieces, weighing each part, and considering every service done or promised, and then decide! Men are continually led astray by misplaced reverence. Shall we be governed by the mere instinct of veneration, uncovering to every man who demands our obeisance? Man is to rule himself, and not be over-mastered by any instinct subordinating the whole to a special part. We ought to know if what we follow be real greatness or seeming greatness; and of the real greatness, of what kind it is, — eminent cunning, eminent intellect, or eminence of religion. For men ought not to gravitate passively, drawn by the bulk of bigness, but consciously and freely to follow eminent wisdom, justice, love, and faith in God. Hence it becomes exceedingly important to study the character of all eminent men; for they represent great social forces for good or ill.

It is true, great men ought to be tried by their peers. But "a cat may look upon a king," and, if she is to enter his service, will do well to look before she leaps. It is dastardly in a democrat to take a master with less scrutiny than he would buy an ox.

Merchants watch the markets: they know what ship brings corn, what hemp, what coal; how much cotton there is at New York or New Orleans; how much gold in the banks. They learn these things, because they live by the market, and seek to get money by their trade. Politicians watch the turn of the people and the coming vote, because they live by the ballot-box, and wish to get honor and office by their skill. So a minister, who would guide men to wisdom, justice, love, and piety, to human welfare, — he must watch the great men, and know what quantity of truth, of justice, of love, and of faith there is in Calhoun, Webster, Clay; because he is to live by the word of God, and only asks, "Thy kingdom come!"

What a great power is a man of large intellect! Aristotle rode on the neck of science for two thousand years, till Bacon, charging down from the vantage-ground of twenty centuries, with giant spear unhorsed the Stagyrite, and mounted there himself; himself in turn to be unhorsed. What a profound influence had Frederick in Germany for half a century! — Napoleon in Europe for the last fifty years! What an influence Sir Robert Peel and Wellington have had in England for the last twenty or thirty years! Jefferson yet leads the democracy of the United States; the dead hand of Hamilton still consolidates the several States. Dead men of great intellect speak from the pulpit. Law is of mortmain. In America it is above all things necessary to study the men of eminent mind, even the men of eminent station; for their power is greater here than elsewhere in Christendom. Money is our only material, greatness our only personal nobility. In England, the influence of powerful men is checked by the great families, the great classes, with their ancestral privileges consolidated into institutions, and the hereditary crown. Here we have no such families; historical men are not from or for such, seldom had historic fathers, seldom leave historic sons. *Tempus ferax hominum, edax hominum.* Fruitful of men is time; voracious also of men.

Even while the individual family continues rich, political unity does not remain in its members, if numerous, more than a single generation. Nay, it is only in families of remarkable stupidity that it lasts a single age.

In this country the swift decay of powerful families is a remarkable fact. Nature produces only individuals, not classes. It is a wonder how many famous Americans leave no children at all. Hancock, and Samuel Adams, Washington, Madison, Jackson — each was a childless flower, that broke off the top of the family tree, which after them dwindled down, and at length died out. It has been so with European stocks of eminent stature. Bacon, Shakspeare, Leibnitz, Newton, Descartes, and Kant died and left no sign. With strange self-complaisance said the first of these, "Great benefactors have been childless men." Here and there an American family continues to bear famous fruit, generation after generation. A single New England tree, rooted far off in the Marches of Wales, is yet green with life, though it has twice blossomed with Presidents; but in general, if the great American leave sons, the wonder is what becomes of them, — so little, they are lost, — a single needle from the American pine, to strew the forest floor amid the other litter of the woods.

No great families here hold great men in check. There is no permanently powerful class. The mechanic is father of the merchant, who will again be the grandsire of mechanics. In thirty years, half the wealth of Boston will be in the hands of men now poor; and, where power of money is of yesterday, it is no great check to any man of large intellect, industry, and will. Here is no hereditary power. So the personal power of a great mind, for good or evil, is free from that three-fold check it meets in other lands, and becomes of immense importance.

Our nation is a great committee of the whole; our State is a provisional government, riches our only heritable good, greatness our only personal nobility; office is elective. To the ambition of a great bad man, or the philanthropy of a great good man, there is no check but the power of money or numbers; no check from great families, great classes, or hereditary privileges. If our man of large intellect runs up hill, there is nothing to check him but the inertia of mankind; if he runs down hill, that also is on his side.

With us the great mind is amenable to no conventional standard measure, as in England or Europe, — only to public opinion. And that public opinion is controlled by money and numbers; for these are the two factors of the American product, the multiplier and the multiplicand, — millions of money, millions of men.

A great mind is like an elephant in the line of ancient battle, — the best ally, if you can keep him in the ranks, fronting the right way; but, if he turn about, he is the fatalest foe, and treads his master underneath his feet. Great minds have a trick of turning round.

Taking all these things into consideration, you see how important it is to scrutinize all the great men, — to know their quantity and quality, — before we allow them to take our heart. To do this is to measure one of the most powerful popular forces for guiding the present and shaping the future. Every office is to be filled by the people's vote, — that of public president and private cook. Franklin introduced new philanthropy to the law of nations. Washington changed men's ideas of political greatness. If Napoleon the Present goes unwhipped of justice, he will change those ideas again; not for the world, but for the saloons of Paris, for its journals and its mob.

How different are conspicuous men to different eyes! The city corporation of Toulouse has just addressed this petition to Napoleon: —

"MONSEIGNIEUR, — The government of the world by Providence is the most perfect. France and Europe style you the elect of God for the accomplishment of his designs. It belongs to no Constitution whatever to assign a term for the divine mission with which you are entrusted. Inspire yourself with this thought, — to restore to the country those tutelar institutions, which form the stability of power and the dignity of nations."

That is a prayer addressed to the Prince President of France, whose private vices are equalled only by his public sins. How different he looks to different men! To me he is Napoleon the Little; to the Mayor and Aldermen of Toulouse, he is the Elect of God, with irresponsible power to rule as long and as badly as likes him best. Well said Sir Philip Sidney, "Spite of the ancients, there is not a piece of wood in the world out of which a Mercury may not be made."

It is this importance of great men which has led me to speak of them so often; not only of men great by nature, but great by position on money or office, or by reputation; men substantially great, and men great by accident. Hence I spoke of Dr. Channing, whose word went like morning over the continents. Hence I spoke of John Quincy Adams, and did not fear to point out every error I thought I discovered in the great man's track, which ended so proudly in the right; and I did homage to all the excellence I found, though it was the most unpopular excellence. Hence I spoke of General Taylor; yes, even of General Harrison, a very ordinary man, but available, and accidentally in a great station. You see why this ought to be done. We are a young nation; a great man easily gives us the impression of his hand; we shall harden in the fire of centuries, and keep the mark. Stamp a letter on Chaldean clay, and how very frail it seems! but burn that clay in the fire, — and, though Nineveh shall perish, and Babylon become a heap of ruins, that brick keeps the arrow-headed letter to this day. As with bricks, so with nations.

Ere long, these three and twenty millions will become a hundred millions; then perhaps a thousand millions, spread over all the continent, from the Arctic to the Antarctic Sea. It is a good thing to start with men of great religion for our guides. The difference between a Moses and a Maximian will be felt by many millions of men, and for many an age, after death has effaced both from the earth. The dead hand of Moses yet circumcises every Hebrew boy; that of mediæval doctors of divinity still clutches the clergyman by the throat; the dead barons of Runnymede even now keep watch, and vindicate for us all a trial by the law of the land, administered by our peers.

A man of eminent abilities may do one of two things in influencing men: either he may extend himself at right angles with the axis of the human march, lateralize himself, spreading widely, and have a great power in his own age, putting his opinion into men's heads, his will into their action, and yet may never reach far onward into the future. In America, he will gain power in his time, by having the common sentiments and ideas, and an extraordinary power to express and show their value; great power of comprehension, of statement, and of will. Such a man differs from others in quantity, not quality. Where all men have considerable, he has a great deal. His power may be represented by two parallel lines, the one beginning where his influence begins, the other where his influence ends. His power will be measured by the length of the lines laterally, and the distance betwixt the parallels. That is one thing.

Or a great man may extend himself forward, in the line of the human march, himself a prolongation of the axis of mankind: not reaching far sideways in his own time, he reaches forward immensely, his influence widening as it goes. He will do this by superiority in sentiments, ideas, and actions; by eminence of justice and of affection; by eminence of religion: he will differ in quality as well as quantity, and have much where the crowd has nothing at all. His power also may be represented by two lines, both beginning at his birth, pointing forwards, diverging from a point, reaching far into the future, widening as they extend, containing time by their stretch, and space by their spread. Jesus of Nazareth was of this class: he spread laterally in his life-time, and took in twelve Galilean peasants and a few obscure women; now his diverging lines reach over two thousand years in their stretch, and contain two hundred and sixty millions of men within their spread.

So much, my friends, and so long, as preface to this estimate of a great man. DANIEL WEBSTER was a man of eminent abilities: for many years the favored son of New England. He was seventy years old; nearly forty years in the councils of the nation; held high office in times of peril and doubt; had a commanding eloquence — there were two million readers for every speech he spoke; and for the last two years he has had a vast influence on the opinion of the North. He has done service; spoken noble words that will endure so long as English lasts. He has largely held the nation's eye. His public office made his personal character conspicuous. Great men have no privacy; their bed and their board are both spread in front of the sun, and their private character is a public force. Let us see what he did, and what he was; what is the result for the present, what for the future.

Daniel Webster was born at Salisbury, N. H. on the borders of civilization, on the 18th of January, 1782. He was the son of Capt. Ebenezer and Abigail Eastman Webster.

The mother of Capt. Webster was a Miss Bachelder, of Hampton, where Thomas Webster, the American founder of the family, settled in 1636. She was descended from the Rev. Stephen Bachiller, formerly of Lynn in Massachusetts, a noted man in his time, unjustly, or otherwise, driven out of the colony by the Puritans. Ebenezer Webster, in his early days, lived as "boy" in the service of Col. Ebenezer Stevens, of Kingston, from whom he received a "lot of land" in Stevenstown, now Salisbury. In 1764 Mr. Webster built himself a log-cabin on the premises, and lighted his fire. His land "lapped on" to the wilderness; no New Englander being so near the North Star, it is said. The family was any thing but rich, living first in a log-cabin, then in a frame-house, and some time keeping tavern.

The father was a soldier of the French war, and in the Revolution; a great, brave, big, brawny man, "high-breasted and broad-shouldered," "with heavy eyebrows," and "a heart which he seemed to have borrowed from a lion;" "a dark man," so black that "you could not tell when his face was covered with gunpowder;" six feet high, and both in look and manners "uncommon rough." He was a shifty man of many functions, — a farmer, a saw-miller, "something of a blacksmith," a captain in the early part of the Revolutionary War, a colonel of militia, representative and senator in the New Hampshire legislature, and finally Judge of the Court of Common Pleas; yet "he never saw the inside of a school-house." In his early married life, food sometimes failed on the rough farm: then the stout man and his neighbors took to the woods, and brought home many a fat buck in their day.

The mother, one of the "black Eastmans," was a quite superior woman. It is often so. When virtue leaps high in the public fountain, you seek for the lofty spring of nobleness, and find it far off in the dear breast of some mother, who melted the snows of winter, and condensed the summer's dew into fair, sweet humanity, which now gladdens the face of man in all the city streets. Bulk is bearded and masculine; niceness is of woman's gendering.

Daniel Webster was fortunate in the outward circumstances of his birth and breeding. He came from that class in society whence almost all the great men of America have come, — the two Adamses, Washington, Hancock, Jefferson, Jackson, Clay, and almost every living notable of our time. New Hampshire herself has furnished a large number of self-reliant and able-headed men, who have fought their way in the world with their own fist, and won eminent stations at the last. The little, rough State breeds professors and senators, merchants and hardy lawyers, in singular profusion. Our Hercules was also cradled on the ground. When he visited the West, a few years ago, an emigrant from New Hampshire met him in Ohio, recognized him, and asked, "Is this the son of Capt. Webster?" "It is, indeed," said the great man. "What!" said he, "is this the little black Dan that used to water the horses?" And the great Daniel Webster said, "It is the little black Dan that used to water the horses." He was proud of his history. If a man finds the way alone, should he not be proud of having found the way, and got out of the woods?

He had small opportunities for academical education. The schoolmaster was "abroad" in New Hampshire; he was seldom at home in Salisbury. Only two or three months in the year was there a school; often only a movable school, that ark of the Lord, shifting from place to place. Sometimes it was two or three miles from Capt. Webster's. Once it was stationary in a log-house. Thither went Daniel Webster, "carrying his dinner in a tin pail," a brave, bright boy: "The child is father of the man." The common-school of America is the cradle of all her greatness. How many Presidents has she therein rocked to vigorous manhood! But Mr. Webster's school-time was much interrupted: there were "chores to be done" at home; the saw-mill to be tended in winter; and, in summer, Daniel "must ride horse to plough;" and in planting-time, and hay-time, and harvest, have many a day stolen from his scanty seed-time of learning. In his father's tavern-barn, the future Secretary gave a rough currying, "after the fashion of the times," to the sorry horse of many a traveller, and in the yard of the inn yoked the oxen of many a New Hampshire teamster. "Cast the bantling on the rocks."

When fourteen years old, he went to Phillips Academy* at Exeter for a few months; then to study with Rev. Mr. Wood at Boscawen, paying a "dollar a week" for the food of the body and for the food of the mind. In the warm weather, "Daniel went barefoot, and wore tow trousers and a tow shirt, his only garments at that season," spun, woven, and made up by his diligent mother. "He helped do the things" about Mr. Wood's barn and wood-pile, and so diminished the pecuniary burthen of his father. But Mr. Wood had small Latin and less Greek, and only taught what he knew. Daniel was an ambitious boy, and apt to learn. Men wonder that some men can do so much with so little outward furniture. The wonder is the other way. He was more college than the college itself, and had a university in his head. It takes time, and the sweat of oxen, and the shouting of drivers, goading and whipping, to get a cart-load of cider to the top of Mount Washington; but the eagle flies there on his own wide wings, and asks no help. Daniel Webster had little academic furniture to help him. He had the mountains of New Hampshire, and his own great mountain of a head. Was that a bad outfit? No millionnaire can buy it for a booby-son.

There was a British sailor, with a wife but no child, an old "man-of-war's-man" living hard by Capt. Webster's, fond of fishing and hunting, of hearing the newspapers read, and of telling his stories to all comers. He had considerable influence on the young boy, and never wore out of his memory.

There was a small social library at Salisbury, whence a bright boy could easily draw the water of life for his intel-

* At the commemoration of Mr. Abbott's fiftieth anniversary as Preceptor of Phillips Academy, a time when "English was of no more account at Exeter than silver at Jerusalem in the days of King Solomon," Mr. Abbott sat between Mr. Webster and Mr. Everett, both of them his former pupils. Mr. John P. Hale, in his neat speech, said, "If you had done nothing else but instruct these two, you might say, EXEGI MONUMENTUM ÆRE PERENNIUS.

lect; at home was the Farmers' Almanac, with its riddles and "poetry," Watts's Hymns and the Bible, the inseparable companion of the New England man. Daniel was fond of poetry, and, before he was ten years old, knew dear old Isaac Watts all by heart. He thought all books were to be got by heart. I said he loved to learn. One day his father said to him, "I shall send you to college, Daniel;" and Daniel laid his head on his father's shoulder, and wept right out. In reading and spelling he surpassed his teacher; but his hard hands did not take kindly to writing, and the schoolmaster told him his "fingers were destined to the plough-tail."

He was not a strong boy, was "a crying baby" that worried his mother; but a neighbor "prophesied," "You will take great comfort in him one day." As he grew up, he was "the slimmest of the family," a farmer's youngest boy, and "not good for much." He did not love work. It was these peculiarities which decided Capt. Webster to send Daniel to college.

The time came for him to go to college. His father once carried him to Dartmouth in a wagon. On the way thither, they passed a spot which Capt. Webster remembered right well. "When you were a little baby," said he, "in the winter we were out of provisions, I went into the woods with the gun to find something to eat. In that spot yonder, then all covered with woods, I found a herd of deer. The snow was very deep, and they had made themselves a *pen*, and were crowded together in great numbers. As they could not get out, I took my choice, and picked out a fine, fat stag. I walked round and looked at him, with my knife in my hand. As I looked the noble fellow in the face, the great tears rolled down his cheeks, and I could not touch him. But I thought of you, Daniel, and your mother, and the rest of the little ones, and carried home the deer."

He can hardly be said to have "entered college:" he only

"broke in," so slenderly was he furnished with elementary knowledge. This deficiency of elementary instruction in the classic tongues and in mathematics was a sad misfortune in his later life.

At college, like so many other New Hampshire boys, he "paid his own way," keeping school in the vacation. One year he paid his board by "doing the literature" for a weekly newspaper. He graduated at Dartmouth in his twentieth year, largely distinguished, though he scorned his degree; and, when the faculty gave him his diploma, he tore it to pieces in the college-yard, in presence of some of his mates, it is said, and trod it under foot.

When he graduated, he was apparently of a feeble constitution, "long, slender, pale, and all eyes," with "teeth as white as a hound's;" thick, black hair clustered about his ample forehead. At first he designed to study theology, but his father's better judgment overruled the thought.

After graduating, he continued to fight for his education, studying law with one hand, keeping school with the other, and yet finding a third hand — this Yankee Briareus — to serve as Register of Deeds. This he did at Fryeburg in Maine, borrowing a copy of Blackstone's Commentaries, which he was too poor to buy. In a long winter-evening, by copying two *deeds*, he could earn fifty cents. He used his money, thus severely earned, to help his older brother, Ezekiel, "Black Zeke," as he was called, to college. Both were "heinously unprovided."

Then he came to Boston, with no letters of introduction, raw, awkward, and shabby in his dress, his rough trousers ceasing a long distance above his feet. He sought admittance as a clerk to more than one office before he found a place; an eminent lawyer, rudely turning him off, "would not have such a fellow in the office!" Mr. Gore, a man of large reputation, took in the unprotected youth, who "came to work, not to play." Here he struggled with poverty and the law. Ezekiel, not yet graduated, came also and took a school in Short-street. Daniel helped his brother in the school. Edward Everett was one of the pupils, a "marvellous boy," with no equal, it was thought, in all New England, making the promise he has since fulfilled.

Mr. Webster was admitted to the bar in 1805, with a prophecy of eminence from Mr. Gore, — a prophecy which might easily be made: such a head was its own fortune-teller. His legal studies over, refusing a lucrative office, he settled down as a lawyer at Boscawen, in New Hampshire. Thence went to Portsmouth in 1807, a lawyer of large talents, getting rapidly into practice; "known all over the State of New Hampshire," known also in Massachusetts. He attended to literature, wrote papers in the Monthly Anthology, a periodical published in the "Athens of America" — so Boston was then called. He printed a rhymed version of some of the odes of Horace, and wrote largely for the "Portsmouth Oracle."

In 1808 he married Miss Grace Fletcher, an attractive and beautiful woman, one year older than himself, the daughter of the worthy minister of Hopkinton, N. H. By this marriage he was the father of two daughters and two sons. But, alas for him! this amiable and beloved woman ceased to be mortal in 1828.

In 1812, when thirty years of age, he was elected to the House of Representatives. In 1814 his house was burned, — a great loss to the young man, never thrifty, and then struggling for an estate. He determined to quit New Hampshire, and seek a place in some more congenial spot. New Hampshire breeds great lawyers, but not great fortunes. He hesitated for a while between Boston and Albany. "He doubted;" so he wrote to a friend, if he "could make a living in Boston." But he concluded to try; and in 1816 he removed to Boston, in the State which had required his ancestor, Rev. Stephen Bachiller, "to forbeare exercising his gifts as a pastor or teacher publiquely in the Pattent," "for his contempt of authority, and till some scandles be removed." *

In 1820, then thirty-eight years old, he is a member of the Massachusetts Convention, and is one of the leading members there; provoking the jealousy, but at the same time distancing the rivalry, of young men Boston born and Cambridge bred. His light, taken from under the New Hampshire bushel at Portsmouth, could not be hid in Boston. It gives light to all that enter the house. In 1822 he was elected to Congress from Boston; in 1827, to the Senate of the United States. In 1841 he was Secretary of State; again a private citizen in 1843; in the Senate in 1845, and Secretary of State in 1850, where he continued, until, "on the 24th of October, 1852, all that was mortal of Daniel Webster was no more!"

He was ten days in the General Court of Massachusetts; a few weeks in her Convention; eight years Representative in Congress; nineteen, Senator; five, Secretary of State. Such is a condensed map of his outward history.

Look next at the Headlands of his life. Here I shall speak of his deeds and words as a citizen and public officer.

He was a great lawyer, engaged in many of the most important cases during the last forty years; but, in the briefness of a sermon, I must pass by his labors in the law.

I know that much of his present reputation depends on his achievements as a lawyer; as an "expounder of the Constitution." Unfortunately, it is not possible for me to say how much credit belongs to Mr. Webster for his constitutional arguments, and how much to the late Judge Story. The publication of the correspondence between these gentle-

* Records of Mass. General Court, Oct. 3, 1632.

men will perhaps help settle the matter; but still much exact legal information was often given by word of mouth, during personal interviews, and that must for ever remain hidden from all but him who gave and him who took. However, from 1816 to 1842, Mr. Webster was in the habit of drawing from that deep and copious well of legal knowledge, whenever his own bucket was dry. Mr. Justice Story was the Jupiter Pluvius from whom Mr. Webster often sought to elicit peculiar thunder for his speeches, and private rain for his own public tanks of law. The statesman got the lawyer to draft bills, to make suggestions, to furnish facts, precedents, law, and ideas. He went on this *aquilician* business, asking aid, now in a "bankruptcy bill," in 1816 and 1825; then in questions of the law of nations, in 1827; next in matters of criminal law in 1830; then of constitutional law in 1832; then in relation to the North-eastern boundary in 1838; in matters of international law again, in his negotiations with Lord Ashburton, in 1842. "You can do more for me than all the rest of the world," wrote the Secretary of State, April 9, 1842, "because you can give me the lights I most want; and, if you furnish them, I shall be confident that they will be true lights. I shall trouble you greatly the next three months." And again, July 16, 1842, he writes, "*Nobody but yourself can do this.*" But, alas! in his later years the beneficiary sought to conceal the source of his supplies. Jupiter Pluvius had himself been summoned before the court of the Higher Law.

Much of Mr. Webster's fame as a Constitutional lawyer rests on his celebrated argument in the Dartmouth College case. But it is easy to see that the facts, the law, the precedents, the ideas, and the conclusions of that argument, had almost all of them been presented by Messrs. Mason and Smith in the previous trial of the case.*

* See the Report of the Case of the Trustees of Dartmouth College, &c. Portsmouth, N. H. [1819.]

Let me speak of the public acts of Mr. Webster in his capacity as a private citizen. Here I shall speak of him chiefly as a public orator.

Two juvenile orations of his are still preserved, delivered while he was yet a lad in college.* One is a fourth of July oration, — a performance good enough for a lad of eighteen, but hardly indicating the talents of its author. The sentiments probably belong to the neighborhood, and the diction to the authorities of the college: —

"Fair Science, too, holds her gentle empire amongst us, and almost innumerable altars are raised to her divinity from Brunswick to Florida. Yale, Providence, and Harvard now grace our land; and DARTMOUTH, towering majestic above the groves which encircle her, now inscribes her glory on the registers of fame! Oxford and Cambridge, those oriental stars of literature, shall now be lost, while the bright sun of American science displays his broad circumference in uneclipsed radiance." — p. 10.

Here is an opinion which he seems to have entertained at the end of his life. He speaks of the formation of the Constitution: —

"We then saw the people of these States engaged in a transaction, which is undoubtedly the greatest approximation towards human perfection the political world ever yet experienced; and which will perhaps for ever stand, in the history of mankind, without a parallel." — p. 8, 9.

---

* "An Oration pronounced at Hanover, N. H. the 4th day of July, 1800, being the Twenty-fourth Anniversary of Independence, by Daniel Webster, member of the Junior Class, Dartmouth University.

> "Do thou, great Liberty, inspire our souls,
> And make our lives in thy possession happy,
> Or our deaths glorious in thy just defence," &c.

"Hanover, 1800." 8vo. pp. 15.

"Funeral Oration, occasioned by the Death of Ephraim Simonds, of Templeton, Mass., a Member of the Senior Class in Dartmouth College, who died at Hanover (N. H.), on the 18th of June, 1801, æt. 26. By Daniel Webster, a class-mate of the deceased. *Et vix sentiunt dicere lingua. Vale.* Hanover, 1801." 8vo. pp. 13.

In 1806, he delivered another Fourth-of-July address at Concord, N. H.,* containing many noble and generous opinions: —

"Patriotism," said he, "hath a source of consolation that cheers the heart in these unhappy times, when good men are rendered odious, and bad men popular; when great men are made little, and little men are made great. A genuine patriot, above the reach of personal considerations, with his eye and his heart on the honor and the happiness of his country, is a character as easy and as satisfactory to himself as venerable in the eyes of the world. While his country enjoys freedom and peace, he will rejoice and be thankful; and, if it be in the councils of Heaven to send the storm and the tempest, he meets the tumult of the political elements with composure and dignity. Above fear, above danger, above reproach, he feels that the last end which can happen to any man never comes too soon, if he fall in defence of the law and the liberty of his country." — p. 21.

In 1812, he delivered a third Fourth-of-July address at Portsmouth.† The political storm is felt in the little harbor of Portsmouth, and the speaker swells with the tumult of the sea. He is hostile to France; averse to the war with England, then waging, yet ready to fight and pay taxes for it. He wants a navy. He comes "to take counsel of the dead," with whom he finds an "infallible criterion." But, alas! "dead men tell no tales," and give no counsel. There was no witch at Portsmouth to bring up Washington quickly.

His subsequent deference to the money-power begins to appear: "The Federal Constitution was adopted for no single reason so much as for the protection of commerce." "Commerce has paid the price of independence." It has been committed to the care of the general government, but "not as a convict to the safe keeping of a jailor," "not for close confinement." He wants a navy to protect it. Such were the opinions of Federalists around him.

* "An Anniversary Address, delivered before the Federal Gentlemen of Concord and its Vicinity, July 4, 1806. By Daniel Webster. Concord, N. H., 1806." 8vo. pp. 21.

† "An Address delivered before the Washington Benevolent Society at Portsmouth, July 4, 1812. By Daniel Webster. Portsm. N. H." 8vo. pp. 27. He delivered also other Fourth-of-July addresses, which I have not seen.

But these speeches of his youth and early manhood were but commonplace productions. In his capacity as public orator, in the vigorous period of his faculties, he made three celebrated speeches, not at all political, — at Plymouth Rock, to celebrate the two hundredth anniversary of New England's birth; at Bunker Hill, in memory of the chief battle of New England; and at Faneuil Hall, to honor the two great men who died when the nation was fifty years old, and they fourscore. Each of these orations was a great and noble effort of patriotic eloquence.

Standing on Plymouth Rock, with the graves of the forefathers around him, how proudly could he say, —

> "Our ancestors established their system of government on morality and religious sentiment. Moral habits, they believed, cannot safely be trusted on any other foundation than religious principle, nor any government be secure which is not supported by moral habits. Living under the heavenly light of revelation, they hoped to find all the social dispositions, all the duties which men owe to each other and to society, enforced and performed. Whatever makes men good Christians makes them good citizens. Our fathers came here to enjoy their religion free and unmolested; and, at the end of two centuries, there is nothing upon which we can pronounce more confidently, nothing of which we can express a more deep and earnest conviction, than of the inestimable importance of that religion to man, both in regard to this life and that which is to come."

At Bunker Hill, there were before him the men of the Revolution, — venerable men who drew swords at Lexington and Concord, and faced the fight in many a fray. There was the French nobleman, — would to God that France had many such to-day! — who perilled his fortune, life, and reputation, for freedom in America, and never sheathed the sword he drew at Yorktown till France also was a republic, — Fayette was there; the Fayette of two revolutions; the Fayette of Yorktown and Olmutz. How well could he say, —

> "Let our conceptions be enlarged to the circle of our duties. Let us extend our ideas over the whole of the vast field in which we are called to

act. Let our object be, OUR COUNTRY, OUR WHOLE COUNTRY, AND NOTHING BUT OUR COUNTRY. And, by the blessing of God, may that country itself become a vast and splendid monument, not of oppression and terror, but of wisdom, of peace, and of liberty, upon which the world may gaze with admiration for ever!"

On another occasion, when two great men, who, in the time that tried men's souls, were of the earliest to peril "their lives, their fortunes, and their sacred honor," — men who, having been one in the Declaration of Independence, were again made one in death, — then the people returned to the cradle wherein the elder Adams and Hancock had rocked Liberty when young; and Webster chaunted the psalm of commemoration to the younger Adams and Jefferson, who had helped that new-born child to walk. He brought before the living the mighty dead; in his words they fought their battles o'er again; we heard them resolve, that, "sink or swim, live or die, survive or perish," they gave their hand and their heart for liberty; and Adams and Jefferson grew greater before the eyes of the people, as he brought them up, and showed the massive services of those men, and pointed out the huge structure of that human fabric which had gone to the grave: —

"Adams and Jefferson, I have said, are no more. As human beings, indeed, they are no more. They are no more, as in 1776, bold and fearless advocates of independence; no more, as at subsequent periods, the head of the government; no more, as we have recently seen them, aged and venerable objects of admiration and regard. They are no more. They are dead. But how little is there of the great and good which can die! To their country they yet live, and live for ever. They live in all that perpetuates the remembrance of men on earth; in the recorded proofs of their own great actions, in the offspring of their intellect, in the deep-engraved lines of public gratitude, and in the respect and homage of mankind. They live in their example; and they live, emphatically, and will live, in the influence which their lives and efforts, their principles and opinions, now exercise, and will continue to exercise, on the affairs of men, not only in their own country, but throughout the civilized world."

How loftily did he say: —

"If we cherish the virtues and the principles of our fathers, Heaven will assist us to carry on the work of human liberty and human happiness. Auspicious omens cheer us. Great examples are before us. Our own firmament now shines brightly upon our path. Washington is in the clear, upper sky. These other stars have now joined the American constellation. They circle round their centre, and the heavens beam with new light. Beneath this illumination let us walk the course of life, and, at its close, devoutly commend our beloved country, the common parent of us all, to the Divine Benignity."

As a political officer, I shall speak of him as a legislator and executor of the law, a maker and administrator of laws.

In November, 1812, Mr. Webster was chosen as Representative to the Thirteenth Congress. At that time the country was at war with Great Britain; and the well-known restraints still fettered the commerce of the country. The people were divided into two great parties,—the Federalists, who opposed the embargo and the war; and the Democrats, who favored both. Mr. Madison, then President, had been forced into the war, contrary to his own convictions of expediency and of right. The most bitter hatred prevailed between the two parties: "party politics were inexpressibly violent." An eminent lawyer of Salem, afterwards one of the most distinguished jurists in the world, a Democrat, was, on account of his political opinions, knocked down in the street, beaten, and forced to take shelter in the house of a friend, whither he fled, bleeding, and covered with the mud of the streets. Political rancor invaded private life; it occupied the pulpit; it blinded men's eyes to a degree almost exceeding belief: were it not now a fact, we should not believe it possible at a former time.

Mr. Webster was a Federalist, earnest and devoted, with the convictions of a Federalist, and the prejudices and the blindness of a Federalist; and, of course, hated by men who had the convictions of a Democrat, and the prejudices and blindness thereof. It is difficult to understand the wilfulness of thorough partisans. In New Hampshire the Judges were Democrats; the Federalists, having a majority in the Legislature, wished to be rid of them, and, for that purpose, abolished all the Courts in the State, and appointed others in their place (1813). I mention this only to show the temper of the times.

There was no great principle of political morals on which the two parties differed, only on measures of expediency. The Federalists demanded freedom of the seas and protection for commerce; but they repeatedly, solemnly, and officially scorned to extend this protection to sailors. They justly complained of the embargo that kept their ships from the sea, but found little fault with the British for impressing sailors from American ships. The Democrats professed the greatest regard for "sailors' rights;" but, in 1814, the government forbade its officers to grant protection to "colored sailors," though Massachusetts had more than a thousand able seamen of that class. Said a leading Federal organ,—"The Union is dear; Commerce is still more dear." "The Eastern States agreed to the Union for the sake of their Commerce."*

With the Federalists there was a great veneration for England. Said Mr. Fisher Ames,—"The immortal spirit of the wood-nymph Liberty dwells only in the British oak." "Our country," quoth he, "is too big for union, too sordid for patriotism, and too democratic for liberty." "England," said another, "is the bulwark of our religion," and the "shield of afflicted humanity." A Federalist newspaper at Boston censured Americans as "enemies of England and monarchy," and accused the Democrats of "antipathy to kingly power." Did Democrats complain that our prisoners were ill-treated by the British, it was declared "foolish and wicked to throw the blame on the British government"! Americans

* "Columbian Centinel" for July 25, 1812.

expressed indignation at the British outrages at Hampton, — burning houses and violating the women. Said the Federal newspapers, it is "impossible that their (the British) military or naval men should be other than magnanimous and humane." Mr. Clay accused the Federalists of "plots that aim at the dismemberment of the Union," and denounced the party as "conspirators against the integrity of the nation."

In general, the Federalists maintained that England had a right to visit American vessels to search for and take her own subjects, if found there; and, if she sometimes took an American citizen, that was only an "incidental evil." Great Britain, said the Massachusetts Legislature, has done us "no essential injury:" she "was fighting the battles of the world." They denied that she had impressed "any considerable number of American seamen." Such was the language of Mr. Webster and the party he served. But even at that time the "Edinburgh Review" declared, "Every American seaman might be said to hold his liberty, and ultimately his life, at the discretion of a foreign commander. In many cases, accordingly, native-born Americans were dragged on board British ships of war: they were dispersed in the remotest quarters of the globe, and not only exposed to the perils of service, but shut out by their situation from all hope of ever being reclaimed. The right of reclaiming runaway seamen was exercised, in short, without either moderation or justice."

Over six thousand cases of impressment were recorded in the American Department of State. In Parliament, Lord Castlereagh admitted that there were three thousand five hundred men in the British fleet claiming to be American citizens, and sixteen hundred of them actually citizens. At the beginning of the war, two thousand five hundred American citizens, impressed into the British navy, refused to fight against their native land, and were shut up in Dartmoor prison. When the Guerrière was captured, there were ten American sailors on board who refused to fight. In Parliament, in 1808, Mr. Baring (Lord Ashburton) defended the rights of Americans against the British orders in council, while in 1812—13 the Federalists could not find out the cases of impressment, — such was the influence of party spirit.

The party out of power is commonly the friend of freedom. The Supreme Court of Massachusetts declared that unconstitutional acts of Congress were void; the Legislature declared it the duty of the State Courts to prevent usurped and unconstitutional powers from being exercised: "It is the duty of the present generation to stand between the next and despotism." "Whenever the national compact is violated, and the citizens of this State oppressed by cruel and unauthorized enactments, this Legislature is bound to interpose its power to wrest from the oppressor his victim."

After the Federal party had taken strong ground, Mr. Webster opposed the administration, opposed the war, took the part of England in the matter of impressment. He drew up the Brentwood Memorial, once so famous all over New England, now forgotten and faded out of all men's memory.*

On the 24th of May, 1813, Mr. Webster first took his seat in the House of Representatives, at the extra session of the thirteenth Congress. He was a member of the Committee on Foreign Affairs, and industriously opposed the administration. In the three sessions of this Congress, he closely followed the leaders of the Federal party; voting with Mr. Pickering a hundred and ninety-one times, and against him only four times, in the two years. Sometimes he "avoided the question;" but voted against thanking Commodore Perry for his naval conduct, against the purchase of Mr. Jefferson's library, against naval supplies, direct taxes, and internal duties.

* I purposely pass over other political writings and speeches of his.

He opposed the government scheme of a National Bank.* No adequate reports of his speeches against the war † are preserved; but, to judge from the testimony of an eminent man, they contained prophetic indications of that oratorical power which was one day so mightily to thunder and lighten in the nation's eyes. Yet his influence in Congress does not appear to have been great. In later years he defended the United States Bank; but that question, like others, had then become a party question; and a horse in the party-team must go on with his fellows, or be flayed by the driver's lash.

But though his labors were not followed by any very marked influence at Washington, at home he drew on himself the wrath of the Democratic party. Mr. Isaac Hill, the editor of the leading Democratic paper in New Hampshire, pursued him with intense personal hatred. He sneeringly says, and falsely, "The great Mr. Webster, so extremely flippant in arguing petty suits in the courts of law, cuts but a sorry figure at Washington: his overweening confidence and zeal cannot *there* supply the place of knowledge." ‡

He was sneeringly called the "great," the "eloquent," the "pre-eminent" Daniel Webster. His deeds, his words, his silence, all were represented as coming from the basest motives, and serving the meanest ends. His journal at Portsmouth was called the "lying oracle." Listen to this: "Mr. Webster spoke much and often when he was in Congress; and, if he had studied the Wisdom of Solomon (as some of his colleagues probably did), he would have discovered that *a fool is known by his much speaking*."

Mr. Webster, in common with his party, refused to take part in the war. "I honor," said he, "the people that

* Speech in the House of Representatives, Jan. 2, 1815. Works, vol. iii. p. 35, *et seq.*

† See his Speech in House of Representatives, Jan. 14, 1814, on the Army Bill. Alexandria, 1814. 8vo. pp. 14.

‡ "New Hampshire Patriot" of July 27, 1813.

shrink from such a contest as this. I applaud their sentiments: they are such as religion and humanity dictate, and such as none but *cannibals* would wish to eradicate from the human heart." Whereupon the editor asks, Will not the federal soldiers call the man who made the speech "a cold-blooded wretch, whose heart is callous to every patriotic feeling?" * and then, "We do not wonder at Mr. Webster's reluctance again to appear at the city of Washington" (he was attending cases at court): "even his native brass must be abashed at his own conduct, at his own speeches." † Flattery "has spoiled him; for application might have made him something a dozen years hence. It has given him confidence, a face of brass, which and his native volubility are mistaken for 'pre-eminent talent.' Of all men in the State, he is the fittest to be the tool of the enemy." ‡ He was one of the men that bring the "nation to the verge of ruin;" a "Thompsonian intriguer;" a "Macfarland admirer." "The self-importance and gross egotism he displays are disgusting." "You would suppose him a great merchant, living in a maritime city, and not a man reared in the *woods* of Salisbury, or educated in the *wilds* of Hanover." §

Before he was elected to Congress, Mr. Hill accused him of "deliberate falsehood," of "telling bold untruths to justify the enormities of the enemy." ‖ The cry was raised, "The Union is in danger." Mr. Webster was to bring about "a dissolution of the Union." ¶ "The few conspirators in Boston, who aim at the division of the Union, and the English Government, who support them in their rebellion, appear to play into each other's hands with remarkable adroitness." The Patriot speaks of "the mad measures of the Boston junto; the hateful, hypocritical scheme of its canting, disaf-

* "New Hampshire Patriot," Aug. 27, 1814.

† *Id.*, Oct. 4, 1814. ‡ *Id.*, Aug. 2, 1814. § *Id.*, Aug. 9, 1814.

‖ *Id.*, Oct. 29, 1812. ¶ *Id.*, Oct. 13, 1812.

fected chief, and the audacious tone of its public prints." * The language of Washington was quoted against political foes; his Farewell Address reprinted. Mr. Webster was charged with "setting the North against the South." The Essex junto was accused of "a plot to destroy the Union," in order "to be under the glorious shelter of British protection." † The Federalists were a "British faction;" the country members of the Massachusetts Legislature were "wooden members;" distinguished characters were "exciting hostility against the Union;" one of these "ought to be tied to the tail of a Congreve rocket, and offered up a burnt sacrifice." It was "moral treason" not to rejoice at the victories of the nation — it was not then "levying war." The Legislature of New Jersey called the acts of the Massachusetts Legislature "the ravings of an infuriated faction," and Gov. Strong a "Maniac Governor." The "Boston Patriot" ‡ called Mr. Webster "the poor fallen Webster," who "curses heartily his setters on:" "the poor creature is confoundedly mortified." Mr. Clay, in Congress, could speak of "the howlings of the whole British pack, let loose from the Essex junto:" the Federalists were attempting "to familiarize the public mind with the horrid scheme of disunion." § And Isaac Hill charges the Federalists with continually "threatening a separation of the States; striving to stir up the passions of the North against the South, — in clear defiance of the dying injunctions of Washington." ‖ I mention these things that all may understand the temper of those times.

In 1814, Mr. Webster sought for the office of Attorney General of New Hampshire, but, failing thereof, was reelected to the House of Representatives. In the fourteenth

* March 30, 1813, quoted from the "Baltimore Patriot."

† "Boston Patriot," No. 1.

‡ July 21, 1813.

§ Speech in House of Representatives, Jan. 8, 1813.

‖ "New Hampshire Patriot" for June 7, 1814.

Congress, two important measures came up amongst others, — the Bank and the Tariff. Mr. Calhoun and Mr. Clay favored the establishment of a national bank, with a capital of $35,000,000. Mr. Webster opposed it by votes and speech, reaffirming the sound doctrines of his former speech: the founders of the Constitution were "hard-money men;" government must not receive the paper of banks which do not pay specie; but "the taxes must be paid in the legal money of the country." * Such was the doctrine of the leading Federalists of the time, and the practice of New England. He introduced a resolution, that all revenues of the United States should be paid in the legal currency of the nation. It met scarce any opposition, and was passed the same day. I think this was the greatest service he ever performed in relation to our national currency or national finance. He was himself proud of it in his later years.†

The protective tariff was supported by Messrs. Calhoun, Clay, and Lowndes. Mr. Webster opposed it; for the capitalists of the North, then deeply engaged in commerce, looked on it as hostile to their shipping, and talked of the "dangers of manufactories." Was it for this reason that the South, always jealous of the Northern thrifty toil, proposed it? So it was alleged.‡ Mr. Webster declared that Congress has no constitutional right to levy duties for protection; only for revenue. Revenue is the constitutional substance; protection, only the accidental shadow. §

In 1816, Mr. Webster removed to Boston. In 1819, while he was a private citizen, a most important question came before the nation, — Shall slavery be extended into the Missouri Territory? Here, too, Mr. Webster was on the

* Speech in House of Representatives, Feb. 28, 1816 (in "National Intelligencer for March 2, 1816). See also Works, vol. iii. p. 35, *et seq.*

† It passed April 26, 1816. Yeas, 79; nays, 35.

‡ But see Mr. Calhoun's defence of his course, Life and Speeches, p. 329.

§ Speech in House of Representatives.

side of freedom. He was one of a committee appointed by a meeting of the citizens of Boston to call a general meeting of the citizens to oppose the extension of slavery. The United States Marshal was chairman of the meeting. Mr. Webster was one of the committee to report resolutions at a subsequent meeting. Said the preamble: —

"The extirpation of slavery has never ceased to be a measure deeply concerning the honor and safety of the United States." "In whatever tends to diminish the evil of slavery, or to check its growth, all parts of the confederacy are alike interested." "If slavery is established in Missouri, then it will be burthened with all the mischiefs which are too well known to be the sure results of slavery; an evil, which has long been deplored, would be incalculably augmented; the whole confederacy would be weakened, and our free institutions disgraced, by the voluntary extension of a practice repugnant to all the principles of a free government, the continuance of which in any part of our country necessity alone has justified."

It was Resolved, that Congress "possesses the constitutional power, upon the admission of any new State created beyond the limits of the original territory of the United States, to make the prohibition of the further extension of slavery or involuntary servitude in such new State, a condition of its admission." "It is just and expedient that this power should be exercised by Congress, upon the admission of all new States created beyond the limits of the original territory of the United States."

In a speech, Mr. Webster "showed incontrovertibly that Congress had this power; that they were called upon by all the principles of sound policy, humanity, and morality, to enact it, and, by prohibiting slavery in the new State of Missouri, oppose a barrier to the further progress of slavery, which else — and this was the last time the opportunity would happen to fix its limits — would roll on desolating the vast expanse of continent to the Pacific Ocean." *

Mr. Webster was appointed chairman of a committee to prepare a memorial to Congress on this matter.† Said he:

* Account of a Meeting at the State House in Boston, Dec. 3, 1819, to consider the Extension of Slavery by the United States (in "Boston Daily Advertiser" for Dec. 4, 1819).

† "A Memorial to the Congress of the United States, on the Subject of Restraining the Increase of Slavery in the New States to be admitted into the Union," &c. &c. Boston, 1819. pp. 22.

"We have a strong feeling of the injustice of any toleration of slavery." But, "to permit it in a new country, what is it but to encourage that rapacity, and fraud, and violence, against which we have so long pointed the denunciations of our penal code? What is it but to tarnish the proud fame of our country? What is it but to throw suspicion on its good faith, and to render questionable all its professions of regard for the rights of humanity and the liberties of mankind?" — p. 21.

At that time, such was the general opinion of the Northern men.* Said a writer in the leading journal of Boston: "Other calamities are trifles compared to this (slavery). War has alleviations; if it does much evil, it does some good: at least, it has an end. But negro-slavery is misery without mixture; it is Pandora's box, but no Hope at the bottom; it is evil, and only evil, and that continually." †

A meeting of the most respectable citizens of Worcester resolved against "any further extension of slavery," as "rendering our boasted Land of Liberty pre-eminent only as a mart for Human Flesh."

"Sad prospects," said the "Boston Daily Advertiser," "indeed for emancipators and colonizers, that, faster than the wit or the means of men can devise a method even for keeping stationary the frightful propagation of slavery, other men, members of the same community, sometimes colleagues of the same deliberative assembly, will be compassing, with all their force, the widest possible extension of slavery." ‡

The South uttered its threat of "dissolving the Union," if slavery were not extended west of the Mississippi. "The

* See a valuable series of papers in the "Boston Daily Advertiser," No. I. to VI., on this subject, from Nov. 20 to Dec. 28, 1819. Charge of Judge Story to the Grand Juries, &c.; *ibid.* Dec. 7 and 8, 1819. Article on the Missouri Compromise, in "North American Review," Jan. 1820. Mr. King's speech in Senate of United States, in "Columbian Centinel" for Jan. 19 and 22, 1820. See also the comments of the "Daily Advertiser" on the treachery of Mr. Mason, the Boston representative, March 28 and 29, 1820.

† "L. M." in "Columbian Centinel" for Dec. 8, 1819.

‡ "Boston Daily Advertiser" for Nov. 20, 1819.

threat," said a writer, "when we consider from whence it comes, raises at once wonder and pity, but has never been thought worth a serious answer here. Even the academicians of Laputa never imagined such a nation as these seceding States would form." "We have lost much; our national honor has received a stain in the eyes of the world; we have enlarged the sphere of human misery and crime."* Only four New Englanders voted for the Missouri Compromise, — Hill and Holmes of Maine, Mason and Shaw of Massachusetts.

Mr. Webster held no public office in this State, until he was chosen a member of the Convention for amending the Constitution of the Commonwealth.

It appears that he had a large influence in the Massachusetts Convention. His speeches, however, do not show any remarkable depth of philosophy, or width of historic view; but they show the strength of a great mind not fully master of his theme. They are not always fair; they sometimes show the specious arguments of the advocate, and do not always indicate the soundness of the judge. He developed no new ideas; looked back more than forward. He stated his opinions with clearness and energy. His leaning was then, as it always was, towards the concentration of power; not to its diffusion. It was the Federal leaning of New England at the time. He had no philosophical objection to a technical religious test as the qualification for office, but did not think it expedient to found a measure on that principle. He wanted property, and not population, as the basis of representation in the Senate. It was "the true basis and measure of power." "Political power," said he, "naturally and necessarily goes into the hands which hold the property." The House might rest on men, the Senate on money. Said he, "It would seem to be the part of political wisdom to found government on property;" yet

* "Boston Daily Advertiser" of March 16, 1820.

he wished to have the property diffused as widely as possible. He was not singular in this preference of money to men. Others thought, that, to put the Senate on the basis of population, and not property, was a change of "an alarming character."

He had small confidence in the people; apparently little sympathy with the multitude of men. He was jealous of the Legislature; afraid of its encroachment on the Judiciary, — New Hampshire had shown him examples of legislative injustice, — but contended ably for the independence of Judges. He had great veneration for the existing Constitution, and thought there would "never be any occasion for great changes" in it, and that "no revision of its general principles would be necessary." Others of the same party thought also that the Constitution was "the most perfect system that human wisdom had ever devised." To judge from the record, Mr. Webster found abler heads than his own in that Convention. Indeed it would have been surprising if a young man, only eight and thirty years of age, should surpass the "assembled wisdom of the State."*

On the 2d of December, 1823, Mr. Webster took his seat in the House of Representatives, as member for Boston. He defended the cause of the Greeks "with the power of a great mind applied to a great subject," denounced the "Holy Alliance," and recommended interference to prevent oppression. Public opinion set strongly in that direction.† "The

* Some valuable passages of Mr. Webster's speeches are omitted from the edition of his Works. (Compare vol. iii. pp. 15 and 17, with the "Journal of Debates and Proceedings in the Convention of Delegates," &c. Boston, 1821. pp. 143, 144, and 145, 146.) A reason for the omission will be obvious to any one who reads the original, and remembers the position and expectations of the author in 1851.

† Meetings had been held in Boston, New York, Philadelphia, and other important towns, and considerable sums of money raised on behalf of the Greeks. Even the educated men were filled with enthusiasm for the descendants of Anacreon and Pericles. The leading journals of England were on the same side. See the letters of John Q. Adams to Mr. Rich and

policy of our Government," said he, "is on the side of liberal and enlightened sentiments." "The civilized world has done with 'the erroneous faith of many made for one.'"* ✓

In 1816 he had opposed a tariff which levied a heavy duty on imports; in 1824 he opposed it again, with vigorous arguments. His speech at that time is a work of large labor, of some nice research, and still of value.† "Like a mighty giant," says Mr. Hayne, "he bore away upon his shoulders the pillars of the temple of error and delusion, escaping himself unhurt, and leaving his adversaries overwhelmed in its ruins." He thought, "the authority of Congress to exercise the revenue-power with direct reference to the protection of manufactures is a questionable authority."‡ He represented the opinion of New England, which "discountenanced the progress of this policy" of high duties. The Federalists of the North inclined to free trade; in 1807 Mr. Dexter thought it "an unalienable right,"§ and in 1820 Judge Story asked why should "the laboring classes be taxed for the necessaries of life?"‖ The tariff of 1824 got but one vote from Massachusetts. As the public opinion of Northern capitalists changed, it brought over the opinion of Mr. Webster, who seems to have had no serious and sober convictions on this subject. At one time the protective system is ruinous to the laboring man, but again "it is aimed point-blank at the protection of labor;" and the duty on coal must not be diminished, lest coal grow

Mr. Luriottis, Dec. 18, 1823; and of John Adams, Dec. 29, 1823. Mr. Clay was on the same side with Mr. Webster. But Mr. Randolph, in his speech in House of Representatives, Jan. 20, 1824, tartly asked, "Why have we never sent an envoy to our sister republic Hayti?"

* See the just and beautiful remarks of Mr. Webster in this speech. Works, vol. iii. pp. 77, 78, and 92 and 93. *Oh si sic semper!*

† Vol. iii. p. 94, *et seq.* See Speech in Faneuil Hall, Oct. 2, 1820.

‡ Speech in reply to Hayne, vol. iii. p. 305.

§ Argument in District Court of Massachusetts against the Embargo.

‖ Memorial of the Citizens of Salem.

scarce and dear.* Non-importation was "an American instinct." †

In 1828 he voted for "the bill of abominations," as that tariff was called, which levied "thirty-two millions of duties on sixty-four millions of imports," "not because he was in favor of the measure, but as the least of two evils."

In 1816 the South wanted a protective tariff: the commercial North hated it. It was Mr. Calhoun‡ who introduced the measure first. Mr. Clay gave it the support of his large talents and immense personal influence, and built up the "American System." Pennsylvania and New York were on that side. Gen. Jackson voted for the tariff of 1824. Mr. Clay was jealous of foreign commerce: it was "the great source of foreign wars." "The predilection of the school of the Essex junto," said he, "for foreign trade and British fabrics is unconquerable." Yet he correctly said, "New England will have the first and richest fruits of the tariff." §

After the system of protection got footing, the Northern capitalists set about manufacturing in good earnest, and then Mr. Webster became the advocate of a high tariff of protective duties. Here he has been blamed for his change of opinion; but to him it was an easy change. He was not a scientific legislator: he had no great and comprehensive ideas of that part of legislation which belongs to political economy. He looked only at the fleeting interest of his constituents, and took their transient opinions of the hour for his norm of conduct. As these altered, his own views also changed. Sometimes the change was a revolution.‖ It

* Works, vol. iv. p. 309. † Works, vol. ii. p. 352.

‡ See Mr. Calhoun's reason for this. Life and Speeches, p. 70, *et seq.*

§ Speech in House of Rep., April 26, 1820. Works, vol. i. p. 150.

‖ Compare his speeches on the tariff in 1824 and 1828 (Works, vol. iii. p. 94, *et seq.*; and 228, *et seq.*) with his subsequent speeches thereon in 1837, 1846. Works, vol. iv. p. 304, *et seq.*; vol. v. p. 361, *et seq.*; and vol. ii. p. 130, *et seq.* and 349, *et seq.* Compare vol. iii. p. 118, *et seq.* and 124, *et seq.* with vol. ii. p. 357. See his reasons for the change of opinion in vol. v. p. 186 and 240. All of these speeches are marked by great ability of statement.

seems to me his first opinion was right, and his last a fatal mistake, that he never answered his first great speech of 1824: but it seems to me that he was honest in the change; for he only looked at the pecuniary interest of his employers, and took their opinions for his guide. But he had other fluctuations on this matter of the tariff, which do not seem capable of so honorable an explanation.*

In the days of nullification, Mr. Webster denied the right of South Carolina to secede from the Union, or to give a final interpretation of the Constitution. She maintained that the Federal Government had violated the Constitution; that she, the aggrieved State of South Carolina, was the judge in that matter, and had a constitutional right to "nullify" the Constitution, and withdraw from the Union.

The question is a deep one. It is the old question of Federal and Democrat, — the question between the constitutional power of the whole, and the power of the parts, — Federal power and State power. Mr. Webster was always in favor of a strong central government; honestly in favor of it, I doubt not. His speeches on that subject were most masterly speeches. I refer, in particular, to that in 1830 against Mr. Hayne, and the speech in 1833 against Mr. Calhoun.

The first of these is the great political speech of Daniel Webster. I do not mean to say that it is just in its political ethics, or deep in the metaphysics of politics, or far-sighted in its political providence. I only mean to say that it surpasses all his other speeches in the massive intellectual power of statement. Mr. Webster was then eight and forty years old. He defended New England against Mr. Hayne; he defended the Constitution of the United States against South Carolina. His speech is full of splendid eloquence; he

* Compare his speech in Faneuil Hall, Sept. 30, 1842, with his tariff speeches in 1846. Works, vol. ii. p. 130, *et seq.* with vol. v. p. 161, *et seq.* and vol. ii. p. 349, *et seq.*

reached high, and put the capstone upon his fame, whose triple foundation he had laid at Plymouth, at Bunker Hill, and at Faneuil Hall. The "republican members of the Massachusetts Legislature" unanimously thanked him for his able vindication of their State. A Virginian, who heard the speech, declared he felt "as if looking at a mammoth treading his native canebrake, and, without apparent consciousness, crushing obstacles which nature had never designed as impediments to him."

He loved concentrated power, and seems to have thought the American Government was exclusively national, and not Federal.* The Constitution was "not a compact." He was seldom averse to sacrificing the claims of the individual States to the claim of the central authority. He favored consolidation of power, while the South Carolinians and others favored local self-government. It was no doctrine of his "that unconstitutional laws bind the people;" but it was his doctrine that such laws bind the people until the Supreme Court declared them unconstitutional; thus making, not the Constitution, but the discretion of the rulers, the measure of its powers.

It is customary at the North to think Mr. Webster wholly in the right, and South Carolina wholly in the wrong, on that question; but it should be remembered, that some of the ablest men whom the South ever sent to Washington thought otherwise. There was a good deal of truth in the speech of Mr. Hayne: he was alarmed at the increase of the central power, which seemed to invade the rights of the States. Mr. Calhoun defended the Carolinian idea; † and Calhoun was a man of great mind, a sagacious man, a man of unimpeach-

* Last remarks on Foote's Resolution, and speech in Senate, 13th Feb. 1833. Works, vol. iii. p. 343, *et seq.*; 448, *et seq.*

† See Mr. Calhoun's Disquisition on Government, and his Discourse on the Constitution and Government of the United States, in his Works, vol. i. (Charleston, 1851); Life and Speeches (New York, 1843), No. iii.—vi. See, too, Life and Speeches, No. ix. xix. xxii.

able integrity in private. Mr. Clay was certainly a man of very large intellect, wise and subtle and far-sighted. But, in 1833, he introduced his "Compromise Measure," to avoid the necessity of enforcing the opinions of Mr. Webster.

I must pass over many things in Mr. Webster's congressional career.

While Secretary of State, he performed the great act of his public life,—the one deed on which his reputation as a political administrator seems to settle down and rest. He negotiated the Treaty of Washington in 1842. The matter was difficult, the claims intricate. There were four parties to pacify,—England, the United States, Massachusetts, and Maine. The difficulty was almost sixty years old. Many political doctors had laid their hands on the immedicable wound, which only smarted sorer under their touch. The British Government sent over a minister to negotiate a treaty with the American Secretary. The two eminent statesmen settled the difficulty. It has been said that no other man in America could have done so well, and drawn the thunder out of the gathered cloud. Perhaps I am no judge of that; yet I do not see why any sensible and honest man could not have done the work. You all remember the anxiety of America and of England; the apprehension of war; and the delight when these two countries shook hands, as the work was done. Then we all felt that there was only one English nation,—the English Briton and the English American; that Webster and Ashburton were fellow-citizens, yea, were brothers of the same great Anglo-Saxon tribe.

His letters on the Right of Search, and the British claim to impress seamen from American ships, would have done honor to any statesman in the world.* He refused to England

* Works, vol. vi. p. 318, *et seq.*

the right to visit and search our ships, on the plea of their being engaged in the slave-trade. Some of my anti-slavery brethren have censured him for this. I always thought he was right in the matter. But, on the other side, his celebrated letter to Lord Ashburton, in the Creole case, seems to me most eminently unjust, false in law, and wicked in morality.* It is the greatest stain on that negotiation; and it is wonderful to me, that, in 1846, Mr. Webster could himself declare that he thought that letter was the most triumphant production from his pen in all the correspondence.

But let us pause a moment, and see how much praise is really due to Mr. Webster for negotiating the treaty. I limit my remarks to the north-eastern boundary. The main question was, Where is the north-west angle of Nova Scotia, mentioned in the treaty of 1783? for a line, drawn due north from the source of the river St. Croix to the summit of the highlands dividing the waters of the Atlantic from those of the St. Lawrence, was to terminate at that point. The American claim was most abundantly substantiated; but it left the British Provinces, New Brunswick and Canada, in an embarrassed position. No military road could be maintained between them; and, besides, the American border came very near to Quebec. Accordingly, the British Government, on the flimsiest pretext, refused to draw the lines and erect the monuments contemplated by the treaty of 1794; perverted the language of the treaty of 1783, which was too plain to be misunderstood; and gradually extended its claim further and further to the west. By the treaty of Ghent (1814), it was provided that certain questions should be left out to a friendly power for arbitration. In 1827, this matter was referred to the King of the Netherlands: he was to determine where the line of the treaty ran. He did not determine that question, but, in 1831, proposed a new conventional line. His award ceded to the British about 4,119 square

* Works, vol. vi. p. 303, *et seq.*

miles of land in Maine. The English assented to it; but the Americans refused to accept the award, Mr. Webster opposing it. He was entirely convinced that the American claim was just and sound, and the American interpretation of the treaty of 1783 the only correct one. On a memorable occasion, in the Senate of the United States, Mr. Webster declared — "that Great Britain ought forthwith to be told, that, unless she would agree to settle the question by the 4th of July next, according to the treaty of 1783, we would then take possession of that line, and let her drive us off if she can!" *

The day before, and in all soberness, he declared that he "never entertained a doubt that the right to this disputed territory was in the United States." This was "perfectly clear, — so clear that the controversy never seemed to him hardly to reach to the dignity of a debatable question."

But, in 1842, the British minister came to negotiate a treaty. Maine and Massachusetts were asked to appoint commissioners to help in the matter; for it seemed determined on that those States were to relinquish some territory to which they had a lawful claim. Those States could not convey the territory to England, but might authorize the Federal Government to make the transfer. The treaty was made, and accepted by Maine and Massachusetts. But it ceded to Great Britain all the land which the award had given, and 893 square miles in addition. Thus the treaty conveyed to Great Britain more than five thousand square miles (upwards of 3,000,000 acres) of American territory, to which, by the terms of the treaty, the American title was perfectly good. Rouse's Point was ceded to the United States, with a narrow strip of land on the north of Vermont and New Hampshire; but the king's award gave us Rouse's Point at less cost. The rights which the Americans gained

* *Evening* Debate of Senate, Feb. 27, 1839 (in "Boston Atlas" of March 1).

with the navigation of a part of the St. John's River were only a fair exchange for the similar right conceded to the British. As a compensation to Maine and Massachusetts for the loss of the land and the jurisdiction over it, the United States paid these two States $300,000, and indemnified Maine for the expenses occasioned by the troubles which had grown out of the contested claims, — about $300,000 more. Great Britain gained all that was essential to the welfare of her colonies. All her communications, civil and military, were for ever placed beyond hostile reach; and all the military positions claimed by America, with the exception of Rouse's Point, were for ever secured to Great Britain. What did England concede? It was fortunate that the controversy was settled; it was wise in America to be liberal. A tract of wild land, though half as large as Massachusetts, is nothing compared to a war. It is as well for mankind that the jurisdiction over that spot belongs to the Lion of England as to the Eagle of America. But I fear a man who makes such a bargain is not entitled to any great glory among diplomatists. In 1832, Maine refused to accept the award of the king, even when the Federal Government offered her a million acres of good land in Michigan, of her own selection, valued at a million and a quarter of dollars. Had it been a question of the south-western boundary, and not the north-eastern, Mexico would have had an answer to her claim very different from that which England received. Mr. Webster was determined on negotiating the treaty at all hazards, and was not very courteous to those who expostulated and stood out for the just rights of Maine and Massachusetts; * nay, he was indignant at the presumption of

* For the facts of this controversy, see, I. The Definitive Treaty of Peace, &c. 1783. Public Statutes of the United States of America (Boston, 1846), vol. viii. p. 80. Treaty of Amity, Commerce, and Navigation, &c. 1794. *ibid.* p. 116. Treaty of Peace and Amity, 1814, *ibid.* p. 218. — II. Act of Twentieth Congress, stat. i. chap. xxx. *id.* vol. iv. p. 262. Act of Twenty-sixth

these States asking for compensation when their land was ceded away! Was there any real danger of a war? If England had claimed clear down to the Connecticut, I think the Southern masters of the North would have given up Bunker Hill and Plymouth Rock, rather than risk to the chances of a British war the twelve hundred million dollars invested in slaves. Men who live in straw houses think twice before they scatter fire-brands abroad. England knew well with whom she had to deal, and authorized her representative to treat only for a "*conventional* line," not to accept the line of the treaty! Mr. Webster succeeded in negotiating, because he gave up more American territory than any one would yield before, — more than the king of the Netherlands had proposed. Still, we may all rejoice in the settlement of the question; and if Great Britain had admitted our claim by the plain terms of the treaty, and then asked for the land so valuable and necessary to her, who in New England would have found fault?

After the conclusion of the treaty, Mr. Webster came to Boston. You remember his speech in 1842, in Faneuil Hall. He was then sixty years old. He had done the great deed of his life. He still held a high station. He scorned, or affected to scorn, the littleness of party and its narrow platform, and claimed to represent the people of the United

Congress, stat. i. chap. lii, *ibid.* vol. v. p. 402; and stat. ii. chap. ii. p. 413. III. Statement, on the part of the United States, of the Case referred in pursuance of the Convention of 29th Sept. 1827, between the said States and Great Britain, to his Majesty the King of the Netherlands, for his decision thereon (Washington, 1829). North American Boundary, A.: Correspondence relating to the Boundary, &c. &c. (London, 1838). North American Boundary, part I.: Correspondence relating to the Boundary, &c. (London, 1840). The Right of the United States of America to the North-Eastern Boundary claimed by them, &c. &c., by Albert Gallatin, &c. (New York, 1840). Documents of the Senate of Massachusetts, 1839, No. 45; 1841, No. 9. Documents of the House of Representatives of the Commonwealth of Massachusetts, 1842, No. 44. — IV. Congressional Globe, &c. (Washington, 1843), vol. xii. and Appendix. Mr. Webster's Defence of the Treaty; Works, vol. v. p. 18, *et seq.*

States. Everybody knew the importance of his speech. I counted sixteen reporters of the New England and Northern press at that meeting. It was a proud day for him, and also a stormy day. Other than friends were about him. It was thought that he had just scattered the thunder which impended over the nation: a sullen cloud still hung over his own expectations of the Presidency. He thundered his eloquence into that cloud, — the great ground-lightning of his Olympian power.

I come now to speak of his relation to slavery. Up to 1850, with occasional fluctuations, much of his conduct had been just and honorable. As a private citizen, in 1819, he opposed the Missouri Compromise. Said he, at the meeting of the citizens of Boston to prevent that iniquity, "We are acting for unborn millions, who lie along before us in the track of time."* The extension of slavery would demoralize the people, and endanger the welfare of the nation. "Nor can the laws derive support from the manners of the people, if the power of moral sentiment be weakened by enjoying, under the permission of the government, great facilities to commit offences." †

A few months after the deed was done, on Forefathers' Day in 1820, standing on Plymouth Rock, he could say: —

"I deem it my duty, on this occasion, to suggest, that the land is not yet wholly free from the contamination of a traffic, at which every feeling of humanity must for ever revolt, — I mean the African slave-trade. Neither public sentiment nor the law has hitherto been able entirely to put an end to this odious and abominable trade. At the moment when God in his mercy has blessed the Christian world with a universal peace, there is reason to fear, that, to the disgrace of the Christian name and character, new efforts are making for the extension of this trade by subjects and citizens of Christian states, in whose hearts there dwell no sentiments of humanity or of justice, and over whom neither the fear of

* Reported in the "Columbian Centinel" for Dec. 8, 1819.

† Memorial to Congress, *ut supra.*

God nor the fear of man exercises a control. In the sight of our law, the African slave-trader is a pirate and a felon; and, in the sight of Heaven, an offender far beyond the ordinary depth of human guilt. There is no brighter page of our history than that which records the measures which have been adopted by the government at an early day, and at different times since, for the suppression of this traffic; and I would call on all the true sons of New England to coöperate with the laws of man and the justice of Heaven. If there be, within the extent of our knowledge or influence, any participation in this traffic, let us pledge ourselves here, upon the rock of Plymouth, to extirpate and destroy it. It is not fit that the land of the Pilgrims should bear the shame longer. I hear the sound of the hammer; I see the smoke of the furnaces where manacles and fetters are still forged for human limbs. I see the visages of those who, by stealth and at midnight, labor in this work of hell, foul and dark, as may become the artificers of such instruments of misery and torture. Let that spot be purified, or let it cease to be of New England. Let it be purified, or let it be set aside from the Christian world. Let it be put out of the circle of human sympathies and human regards; and let civilized man henceforth have no communion with it."

In 1830, he honored Nathan Dane for the Ordinance which makes the difference between Ohio and Kentucky, and honorably vindicated that man who lived "too near the north star" for Southern eyes to see. "I regard domestic slavery," said Mr. Webster to Mr. Hayne, "as one of the greatest evils, both moral and political." *

In 1837, at Niblo's Garden, he avowed his entire unwillingness to do any thing that should extend the slavery of the African race on this continent. Said he: —

"On the general question of slavery, a great portion of the community is already strongly excited. The subject has not only attracted attention as a question of politics, but it has struck a far deeper-toned chord. It has arrested the religious feeling of the country; it has taken strong hold on the consciences of men. He is a rash man, indeed, and little conversant with human nature, — and especially has he a very erroneous estimate of the character of the people of this country, — who supposes that a feeling of this kind is to be trifled with or despised. It will assuredly cause itself to be respected. It may be reasoned with; it may be made willing — I believe it is entirely willing — to fulfil all existing

* Works, vol. iii. p. 279; see also p. 263, *et seq.*

States. Everybody knew the importance of his speech. I counted sixteen reporters of the New England and Northern press at that meeting. It was a proud day for him, and also a stormy day. Other than friends were about him. It was thought that he had just scattered the thunder which impended over the nation: a sullen cloud still hung over his own expectations of the Presidency. He thundered his eloquence into that cloud, — the great ground-lightning of his Olympian power.

I come now to speak of his relation to slavery. Up to 1850, with occasional fluctuations, much of his conduct had been just and honorable. As a private citizen, in 1819, he opposed the Missouri Compromise. Said he, at the meeting of the citizens of Boston to prevent that iniquity, " We are acting for unborn millions, who lie along before us in the track of time."* The extension of slavery would demoralize the people, and endanger the welfare of the nation. " Nor can the laws derive support from the manners of the people, if the power of moral sentiment be weakened by enjoying, under the permission of the government, great facilities to commit offences." †

A few months after the deed was done, on Forefathers' Day in 1820, standing on Plymouth Rock, he could say: —

" I deem it my duty, on this occasion, to suggest, that the land is not yet wholly free from the contamination of a traffic, at which every feeling of humanity must for ever revolt, — I mean the African slave-trade. Neither public sentiment nor the law has hitherto been able entirely to put an end to this odious and abominable trade. At the moment when God in his mercy has blessed the Christian world with a universal peace, there is reason to fear, that, to the disgrace of the Christian name and character, new efforts are making for the extension of this trade by subjects and citizens of Christian states, in whose hearts there dwell no sentiments of humanity or of justice, and over whom neither the fear of

---

* Reported in the " Columbian Centinel " for Dec. 8, 1819.

† Memorial to Congress, *ut supra.*

Quincy Adams, but, alas! did too little to oppose that annexation. Against him were Mr. Calhoun, the South, almost all the Democratic party of the North; Mr. Van Buren losing his nomination on account of his hostility to new slave-soil; and many of the capitalists of the North wished a thing that Mr. Webster wanted not.

He objected to the Constitution of Texas. Why? Because it tied up the hands of the Legislature against the abolition of slavery. He said so on Forefathers' Day, two hundred and twenty-five years after the landing of the Pilgrims on Plymouth Rock. Then he could not forget his own proud words, uttered a quarter of a century before. I thought him honest then; I think so still. But he said that New England might have prevented annexation; that Massachusetts might have prevented annexation, only "she could not be roused." If he had labored then for freedom with as much vigor and earnestness as he wrought for slavery in 1850 and 1851, Massachusetts would have been roused, New England would have risen as a single man, and annexation of new slave-soil have been put off till the Greek Kalends, a day beyond eternity. Yet he did some service in this work.

After the outbreak of the Mexican war, the northern men sought to pass a law prohibiting slavery in the new territory gained from Mexico. The celebrated "Wilmot proviso" came up. Mr. Webster also wished to prohibit slavery in the new territory. In March, 1847, he presented to Congress the resolutions of the Massachusetts Legislature against the extension of slavery,—which had been passed unanimously,—and he endorsed them all.

> "I thank her for it, and am proud of her; for she has denounced the whole object for which our armies are now traversing the mountains of Mexico." "If any thing is certain, it is that the sentiment of the whole North is utterly opposed to the acquisition of territory to be formed into new Slave-holding States." *

---

* "Congressional Globe," March, 1847, p. 555.

At the Whig Convention at Springfield, in 1847, he maintained that the Wilmot Proviso was his "thunder."

"Did I not commit myself in 1837 to the whole doctrine, fully, entirely?" "I cannot quite consent that more recent discoverers should claim the merit and take out a patent. We are to use the first and the last and every occasion which offers to oppose the extension of slave power."*

On the 10th of August, 1848, in the Senate of the United States, he said: —

"My opposition to the increase of slavery in this country, or to the increase of slave-representation, is general and universal. It has no reference to the lines of latitude or points of the compass. I shall oppose all such extension at all times and under all circumstances, even against all inducements, against all supposed limitations of great interests, against all combinations, against all compromises."

He sought to gain the support of the Free Soilers in Massachusetts, and encouraged their enterprise. Even when he denounced the nomination of General Taylor as "not fit to be made," he declared that he could stand on the Buffalo Platform; its Anti-Slavery planks were good sound Whig timber; he himself had had some agency in getting them out, and did not see the necessity of a new organization.

But, alas! all this was to pass away. Was he sincere in his opposition to the extension of slavery? I always thought so. I think so still. But how inconsistent his conduct!

Yet, after all, on the 7th of March, 1850, he could make that speech — you know it too well. He refused to exclude slavery by law from California and New Mexico. It would "irritate" the South, would "re-enact the law of God." He declared Congress was bound to make four new Slave States out of Texas; to allow all the territory below 36° 30′ to become Slave States; he declared that he would give Texas fifty thousand square miles of land for slave-territory, and ten millions of dollars; would refund to Virginia two hundred millions of dollars derived from the sales

* Remarks in Convention at Springfield, Sept. 10, 1847; reported in "Boston Daily Advertiser."

of the public lands, to expatriate the free colored people from her soil; that he would support the Fugitive Slave Bill, with all its amendments, "with all its provisions," "to the fullest extent."

You know the Fugitive Slave Bill too well. It is bad enough now; but when he first volunteered his support thereto, it was far worse, for then every one of the seventeen thousand postmasters of America might be a legal kidnapper by that Bill. He pledged our own Massachusetts to support it, and that "with alacrity."

My friends, you all know the speech of the 7th of March: you know how men felt when the telegraph brought the first news, they thought there must be some mistake! They could not believe the lightning. You know how the Whig party, and the Democratic party, and the newspapers, treated the report. When the speech came in full, you know the effect. One of the most conspicuous men of the State, then in high office, declared that Mr. Webster "seemed inspired by the devil to the extent of his intellect." You know the indignation men felt, the sorrow and anguish. I think not a hundred prominent men in all New England acceded to the speech. But such was the power of that gigantic intellect, that, eighteen days after his speech, nine hundred and eighty-seven men of Boston sent him a letter, telling him that he had pointed out "the path of duty, convinced the understanding and touched the conscience of a nation;" and they expressed to him their "entire concurrence in the sentiments of that speech," and their "heartfelt thanks for the inestimable aid it afforded to the preservation" of the Union.

You remember the return of Mr. Webster to Boston; the speech at the Revere House; his word that "discussion" on the subject of slavery must "in some way be suppressed;" you remember the "disagreeable duty;" the question if Massachusetts "will be just against temptation;" whether "she will conquer her prejudices" in favor of the trial by jury, of the unalienable rights of man, in favor of the Christian religion, and "those thoughts which wander through eternity."

You remember the agony of our colored men. The Son of man came to Jerusalem to seek and to save that which was lost; but Daniel Webster came to Boston to crush the poorest and most lost of men into the ground with the hoof of American power.

At the moment of making that speech, Mr. Webster was a member of a French Abolition Society, which has for its object to protect, enlighten, and emancipate the African race! *

You all know what followed. The Fugitive Slave Law Bill passed. It was enforced. You remember the consternation of the colored people in Boston, New York, Buffalo, Philadelphia, — all over the land. You remember the speeches of Mr. Webster at Buffalo, Syracuse, and Albany, — his industry, never equalled before; his violence, his indignation, his denunciations. You remember the threat at Syracuse, that out of the bosom of the next Anti-slavery Convention should a fugitive slave be seized. You remember the scorn that he poured out on men who pledged "their lives, their fortunes, and their sacred honor," for the welfare of men.

You remember the letters to Mr. Webster from Newburyport, Kennebec, Medford, and his "Neighbors in New Hampshire." You have not forgotten the "Union Meetings:" "Blue-light Federalists," and "Genuine Democrats dyed in the wool," united into one phalanx of Hunkerism and became his "retainers," lay and clerical, — the laymen maintaining that his political opinions were an amendment to the Constitution; and the clergymen, that his public and

* Institut d'Afrique pour l'Abolition de la Traite et de l'Esclavage. Art. ii. "Il a pour but également de protéger, d'éclairer et d'émanciper la race Africaine."

private practice was one of the evidences of Christianity. You remember the sermons of Doctors of Divinity, proving that slavery was Christian, good Old Testament Christian, at the very least. You remember the offer of a man to deliver up his own brother. Andover went for kidnapping. The loftiest pulpits, — I mean those highest bottomed on the dollar, — they went also for kidnapping. There went up a shout against the fugitive from the metropolitan pulpits, "Away with such a fellow from the earth! — Kidnap him, kidnap him!" And when we said, mildly remonstrating, "Why, what evil has the poor black man done?" the answer was, — "We have a law, and by that law he ought to be a slave!"

You remember the first kidnappers which came here to Boston. Hughes was one of them, an ugly-looking fellow, that went back to die in a street-brawl in his own Georgia. He thirsted for the blood of Ellen Craft.

You remember the seizure of Shadrach; you remember his deliverance out of his fiery furnace. Of course it was an Angel who let him out; for that court, — the kidnappers' court, — thirsting for human blood, spite of the "enlargement of the testimony," after six trials, I think, has not found a man, who, at noonday and in the centre of the town, did the deed. So I suppose it was an Angel that did the deed, and miracles are not over yet. I hope you have not forgotten Caphart, the creature which "whips women," the great ally of the Boston kidnappers.

You remember the kidnapping of Thomas Sims; Faneuil Hall shut against the convention of the people; the court-house in chains; the police drilled in the square; soldiers in arms; Faneuil Hall a barrack. You remember Fast Day, 1851, — at least I do. You remember the "Acorn" and Boston on the 12th of April. You have not forgotten the dreadful scenes at New York, Philadelphia, and Buffalo; the tragedy at Christiana.

You have not forgotten Mr. Webster's definition of the object of government. In 1845, standing over the grave of Judge Story, he said, — "Justice is the great interest of mankind." I think he thought so too; but at New York, on the 18th of November, 1850, he said, — "The great object of government is the protection of property at home, and respect and renown abroad."

He went to Annapolis, and made a speech complimenting a series of ultra-resolutions in favor of slavery and slave-catching. One of the resolutions made the execution of the Fugitive Slave Law the sole bond of the Union. The orator of Bunker Hill replied: —

"Gentlemen, I concur in the sentiments expressed by you all — and I thank God they were expressed by you all — in the resolutions passed here on the 10th of December. And allow me to say, that any State, North or South, which departs *one iota* from the sentiment of that resolution, is disloyal to this Union.

"Further, — so far as any act of that sort has been committed, — SUCH A STATE HAS NO PORTION OF MY REGARD. *I do not sympathize with it.* I rebuke it wherever I speak, and on all occasions where it is proper for me to express my sentiments. . If there are States — and I am afraid there are — which have sought, by ingenious contrivances of State legislation, to thwart the fair exercise and fulfilment of the laws of Congress passed to carry into effect the compacts of the Constitution, — THAT STATE, SO FAR, IS ENTITLED TO NO REGARD FROM ME. AT THE NORTH THERE HAVE BEEN CERTAINLY SOME INTIMATIONS IN CERTAIN STATES OF SUCH A POLICY."

"*I hold the importance of maintaining these measures to be of the highest character and nature, every one of them out and out, and through and through. I have no confidence in anybody who seeks the repeal, in anybody who wishes to alter or modify these constitutional provisions.* There they are. Many of these great measures are irrepealable. The settlement with Texas is as irrepealable as the admission of California. Other important objects of legislation, if not in themselves in the nature of grants, and therefore not so irrepealable, are just as important; and *we are to hear no parleying upon it. We are to listen to no modification or qualification.* They were passed in conformity with the provisions of the Constitution; *and they must be performed and abided by,* IN WHATEVER EVENT, AND AT WHATEVER COST."

Surrounded by the Federalists of New England, when a

young man, fresh in Congress, he stood out nobly for the right to discuss all matters. Every boy knows his brave words by heart: —

"Important as I deem it, sir, to discuss, on all proper occasions, the policy of the measures at present pursued, *it is still more important to maintain the right of such discussion in its full and just extent.* Sentiments lately sprung up, and now growing popular, render it necessary to be explicit on this point. It is the ancient and constitutional right of this people to canvass public measures, and the merits of public men. It is a homebred right, a fireside privilege. It has ever been enjoyed in every house, cottage, and cabin in the nation. It is not to be drawn into controversy. It is as undoubted as the right of breathing the air, and walking on the earth. Belonging to private life as a right, it belongs to public life as a duty; and it is the last duty which those whose representative I am shall find me to abandon. This high constitutional privilege I shall defend and exercise within this house and without this house, and in all places; in time of war, in time of peace, and at all times.

"Living, I will assert it; dying, I will assert it; and should I leave no other inheritance to my children, by the blessing of God I will leave them the inheritance of *Free Principles*, and the example of a manly, independent, and constitutional defence of them."

Then, in 1850, when vast questions, so intimately affecting the welfare of millions of men, were before the country, he told us to suppress agitation!

"Neither you nor I shall see the legislation of the country proceed in the old harmonious way, until the discussions in Congress and out of Congress upon the subject [of slavery] shall be in some way suppressed. Take that truth home with you, and take it as truth."

"I shall support no agitations having their foundation in unreal and ghostly abstractions."*

The opponents of Mr. Webster, contending for the freedom of all Americans, of all men, appealed from the Fugitive Slave Bill to "the element of all laws, out of which they are derived, to the end of all laws, for which they are designed and in which they are perfected." How did he resist the appeal? You have not forgotten the speech at Capron Springs, on the 26th of June, 1851. "When noth-

* Speech at the Revere House in Boston, April 29, 1850, in "Daily Advertiser" of April 30.

ing else will answer," says he, "they," the abolitionists, "invoke religion, and speak of the 'higher law!'" He of the granite hills of New Hampshire, looking on the mountains of Virginia, blue with loftiness and distance, said, "Gentlemen, this North Mountain is high, the Blue Ridge higher still, the Alleghanies higher than either, and yet this 'higher law' ranges further than an eagle's flight above the highest peaks of the Alleghanies! No common vision can discern it; no common and unsophisticated conscience can feel it; the hearing of common men never learns its high behests; and, therefore, one would think it is not a safe law to be acted upon in matters of the highest practical moment. It is the code, however, of the abolitionists of the North."

This speech was made at dinner. The next "sentiment" given after his was this: —

> "*The Fugitive Slave Law* — Upon its faithful execution depends the perpetuity of the Union."

Mr. Webster made a speech in reply, and distinctly declared, —

> "You of the South have as much right to secure your fugitive slaves, as the North has to any of its rights and privileges of navigation and commerce."

Do you think he believed that? Daniel Webster knew better. In 1844, only seven years before, he had said, —

> "What! when all the civilized world is opposed to slavery; when morality denounces it; when Christianity denounces it; when every thing respected, every thing good, bears one united witness against it, is it for America — America, the land of Washington, the model republic of the world — is it for America to come to its assistance, and to insist that the maintenance of slavery is necessary to the support of her institutions?"

How do you think the audience answered then? With six and twenty cheers. It was in Faneuil Hall. Said Mr. Webster, "These are Whig principles;" and, with these, "Faneuil Hall may laugh a siege to scorn." That speech is not printed in his collection! How could it stand side by side with the speech of the 7th of March?

In 1846, a Whig Convention voted to do its possible to "defeat all measures calculated to uphold slavery, and promote all constitutional measures for its overthrow;" to "oppose any further addition of Slaveholding States to this Union;" and to have "free institutions for all, chains and fetters for none."

Then Mr. Webster declared he had a heart which beat for every thing favorable to the progress of human liberty, either here or abroad; then, when in "the dark and troubled night" he saw only the Whig party as his Bethlehem Star, he rejoiced in "the hope of obtaining the power to resist whatever threatens to extend slavery." * Yet after New York had kidnapped Christians, and with civic pomp sent her own sons into slavery, he could go to that city and say, "It is an air which for the last few months I love to inhale. It is a patriotic atmosphere: constitutional breezes fan it every day." †

To accomplish a bad purpose, he resorted to mean artifice, to the low tricks of vulgar adventurers in politics. He used the same weapons once wielded against him,—misrepresentation, denunciation, invective. Like his old enemy of New Hampshire, he carried his political quarrel into private life. He cast off the acquaintance of men intimate with him for twenty or thirty years. The malignity of his conduct, as it was once said of a great apostate, "was hugely aggravated by those rare abilities whereof God had given him the use." Time had not in America bred a man before bold enough to consummate such aims as his. In this New Hampshire Strafford, "despotism had at length obtained an instrument with mind to comprehend, and resolution to act upon, its principles in their length and breadth; and enough of his

* Speech at Faneuil Hall, Sept. 23, 1846, reported in the "Daily Advertiser," Sept. 24.

† Speech at New York, May 12, 1851, in "Boston Atlas" of May 14.

purposes were effected by him to enable mankind to see as from a tower the end of all."

What was the design of all this? It was to "save the Union." Such was the cry. Was the Union in danger? Here were a few non-resistants at the North, who said, We will have "no union with slaveholders." There was a party of seceders at the South, who periodically blustered about disunion. Could these men bring the Union into peril? Did Daniel Webster think so? I shall never insult that giant intellect by the thought. He knew South Carolina, he knew Georgia, very well.* Mr. Benton knew of no "distress," even at the time when it was alleged that the nation was bleeding at "five gaping wounds," so that it would take the whole Omnibus full of compromises to stanch the blood: "All the political distress is among the politicians."† I think Mr. Webster knew there was no danger of a dissolution of the Union. But here is a proof that he knew it. In 1850, on the 22d of December, he declared, "There is no longer imminent danger of the dissolution of the United States. We shall live, and not die." But, soon after, he went about saving the Union again, and again, and again,— saved it at Buffalo, Albany, Syracuse, at Annapolis, and then at Capron Springs.

I say there was no real danger; but my opinion is a mere opinion, and nothing more. Look at a fact. We have the most delicate test of public opinion,—the state of the public funds; the barometer which indicates any change in the political weather. If the winds blow down the Tiber, Roman funds fall. Talk of war between France and England, the stocks go down at Paris and London. The foolish talk about the fisheries last summer lowered American stocks in the market, to the great gain of prudent and far-sighted brokers, who knew there was no danger. But all this time, when Mr.

* See his description in 1830 of the process and conclusion of nullification. Works, vol. iii. p. 337, *et seq.*

† Speech in Senate, Sept. 10, 1850.

Webster was telling us the ship of state was going to pieces, and required undergirding by the Fugitive Slave Bill, and needed the kidnapper's hand at the helm; while he was advising Massachusetts to "conquer her prejudices" in favor of the unalienable rights of man; while he was denouncing the friends of freedom, and calling on us to throw over to Texas — the monster of the deep that threatened to devour the ship of state — fifty thousand square miles of territory, and ten millions of dollars; and to the other monster of secession to cast over the trial by jury, the dearest principles of the Constitution, of manhood, of justice, and of religion, "those thoughts that wander through eternity;" while he himself revoked the noblest words of his whole life, throwing over his interpretation of the Constitution, his respect for State rights, for the common law, his own morality, his own religion, and his own God, — the funds of the United States did not go down one mill. You asked the capitalist, "Is the Union in danger?" He answered, "O yes! it is in the greatest peril." "Then will you sell me your stocks lower than before?" "Not a mill; not one mill — not the ten hundredth part of a dollar in a hundred!" To ask men to make such a sacrifice, at such a time, from such a motive, is as if you should ask the captain of the steamer "Niagara," in Boston harbor, in fair weather, to throw over all his cargo, because a dandy in the cabin was blowing the fire with his breath. No, my friends, I shall not insult the majesty of that intellect with the thought that he believed there was danger to the Union. There was not any danger of a storm; not a single cat's-paw in the sky; not a capful of bad weather between Cape Sable and the Lake of the Woods!

But suppose the worst came to the worst, are there no other things as bad as disunion? The Constitution — does it "establish justice, ensure domestic tranquillity," and "secure the blessings of liberty" to all the citizens? Nobody pretends it, — with every sixth man made merchandise, and not an inch of free soil covered by the Declaration of Independence, save the five thousand miles which Mr. Webster ceded away. Is disunion worse than slavery? Perhaps not even to commerce, which the Federalists thought "still more dear" than Union. But what if the South seceded next year, and the younger son took the portion of goods that falleth to him, when America divides her living? Imagine the condition of the new nation, — the United States South; a nation without schools, or the desire for them; without commerce, without manufactures; with six million white men and three million slaves; working with that barbarous tool, slave-labor, an instrument as ill-suited to these times as a sickle of stone to cut grain with! How would that new democracy appear in the eyes of the world, when the public opinion of the nations looks hard at tyranny? It would not be long before this younger son, having spent all with riotous living, and devoured his substance with slavery, brought down to the husks that the swine do eat, — would arise, and go to his father, and say, "Father, forgive me; I have sinned against heaven and in thy sight, and am no more worthy to be called thy son. Make me as one of thy hired servants." The Southern men know well, that, if the Union were dissolved, their riches would take to itself legs, and run away, — or firebrands, and make a St. Domingo out of Carolina! They cast off the North! they set up for themselves! "Tush! tush! Fear boys with bugs!"

Here is the reason. He wanted to be President. That was all of it. Before this he had intrigued, — always in a clumsy sort, for he was organized for honesty, and cunning never throve in his keeping, — had stormed and blustered and bullied. "Gen. Taylor the second choice of Massachusetts for the President," quoth he: "I tell you I am to be the first, and Massachusetts has no second choice." Mr. Clay must not be nominated in '44; in '48 Gen. Taylor's was a "nomination not fit to be made." He wanted the office himself. This time he must storm the North, and conciliate the South. This was his bid for the Presidency, — fifty thousand square miles of territory and ten millions of dollars to Texas; four new Slave States; slavery in Utah and New Mexico; the Fugitive Slave Bill; and two hundred millions of dollars offered to Virginia to carry free men of color to Africa.

He never labored so before, and he had been a hard-working man. What speeches he made at Boston, New York, Philadelphia, Albany, Buffalo, Syracuse, Annapolis! What letters he wrote! His intellect was never so active, nor gave such proofs of Herculean power. The hottest headed Carolinian did not put his feet faster or further on in the support of slavery. He

> "Stood up the strongest and the fiercest spirit
> That fought 'gainst Heaven, now fiercer by despair."

Once he could say,—

> "By general instruction, we seek as far as possible to purify the whole moral atmosphere; to keep good sentiments uppermost, and to turn the strong current of feeling and opinion, as well as the censures of the law, and the denunciations of religion, against immorality and crime. We hope for a security beyond the law, and above the law, in the prevalence of enlightened and well-principled moral sentiment." *

In 1820 he could say, "All conscience ought to be respected;" in 1850 it is only a fanatic who heeds his conscience, and there is no higher law. In scorn of the higher law, he far outwent his transatlantic prototype. Even Strafford, in his devotion to "*Thorough*," had some respect for the fundamental law of nature, and said,—"If I must be a traitor to man or perjured to God, I will be faithful to my Creator."

The fountains of his great deep were broken up — it rained forty days and forty nights, and brought a flood of slavery over this whole land; it covered the market, and the factory,

* Debate in the Mass. Convention, Dec. 5, 1820. "Journal," *ubi sup.* p. 145; erroneously printed 245.

and the court-house, and the warehouse, and the college, and rose up high over the tops of the tallest steeples! But the Ark of Freedom went on the face of the waters, — above the market, above the factory, above the court-house, over the college, higher than the tops of the tallest steeples, it floated secure; for it bore the Religion that is to save the world, and the Lord God of Hosts had shut it in.

What flattery was there from Mr. Webster! What flattery to the South! what respect for Southern nullifiers! "The Secessionists of the South take a different course of remark;" they appeal to no higher law! "They are learned and eloquent; they are animated and full of spirit; they are high-minded and chivalrous; they state their supposed injuries and causes of complaint in elegant phrases and exalted tones of speech." *

He derided the instructions of his adopted State.

"It has been said that I have, by the course that I have thought proper to pursue, displeased a portion of the people of Massachusetts. Well, suppose I did. Suppose I displeased all the people of that State, — what of that?

"What had I to do with instructions from Massachusetts upon a question affecting the whole nation!" "I assure you, gentlemen, I cared no more for the instructions of Massachusetts than I did for those of any other State!" †

What scorn against the "fanatics" of the North, against the Higher Law, and the God thereof!

"New England, it is well known, is the chosen seat of the Abolition presses and the Abolition Societies. There it is principally that the former cheer the morning by full columns of lamentation over the fate of human beings free by nature and by a law above the Constitution, — but sent back, nevertheless, chained and manacled to slavery and to stripes; and the latter refresh themselves from daily toil by orgies of the night devoted to the same outpourings of philanthropy, mingling all the while their anathemas at what they call 'men-catching' with the most horrid and profane abjuration of the Christian Sabbath, and indeed of the whole

---

* Speech at Capron Springs. † Ibid.

Divine Revelation: they sanctify their philanthropy by irreligion and profanity; they manifest their charity by contempt of God and his commandments."

"Depend upon it, the law [the Fugitive Slave Bill] will be executed in its spirit and to its letter. It will be executed in all the great cities, — here in Syracuse, — in the midst of the next Anti-slavery Convention, if the occasion shall arise; then we shall see what becomes of their 'lives and their sacred honor'!" *

How he mocked at the "higher law," "that exists somewhere between us and the third heaven, I never knew exactly where."

The anti-slavery men were "insane persons," "some small bodies of fanatics," "not fit for a lunatic asylum." †

To secure his purposes, he left no stone unturned; he abandoned his old friends, treating them with rage and insolence. He revolutionized his own morals, and his own religion. The strong advocate of liberty, of justice to all men, the opponent of slavery, turned round and went square over. But his old speeches did not follow him: a speech is a fact; a printed word becomes immovable as the Alps. His former speeches, all the way from Hanover to Washington, were a line of fortresses grim with cannon each levelled at his new position.

How low he stooped to supplicate the South, to cringe before the Catholics, to fawn upon the Methodists at Faneuil Hall! Oh, what a prostitution of what a kingly power of thought, of speech, of will!

The effect of Mr. Webster's speech was amazing: at first Northern men abhorred it; next they accepted it. Why was this? He himself has perhaps helped us understand the mystery: —

"The enormity of some crimes so astonishes men as to subdue their minds, and they lose the desire for justice in a morbid admiration of the great criminal and the strangeness of the crime."

---

* Speech at Syracuse (New York, 1851).

† See speech at Buffalo, 22d May, 1851. Vol. ii. p. 544, *et seq.*

Slavery, the most hideous snake which Southern regions breed, with fifteen unequal feet, came crawling North; fold on fold, and ring on ring, and coil on coil, the venomed monster came: then Avarice, the foulest worm which Northern cities gender in their heat, went crawling South; with many a wriggling curl, it wound along its way. At length they met, and, twisting up in their obscene embrace, the twain became one monster, Hunkerism; theme unattempted yet in prose or song: there was no North, no South; they were one poison! The dragon wormed its way along, — crawled into the church of commerce, wherein the minister baptized the beast, "Salvation." From the ten commandments the dragon's breath effaced those which forbid to kill and covet, with the three between; then, with malignant tooth, gnawed out the chief commandments whereon the law and prophets hang. This amphisbæna of the Western World then swallowed down the holiest words of Hebrew or of Christian speech, and in their place it left a hissing at the higher law of God. Northward and Southward wormed the thing along its track, leaving the stain of its breath in the people's face; and its hissing against the Lord rings yet in many a speech:

"Religion, blushing, veils her sacred fires,
And, unawares, morality expires."

Then what a shrinking was there of great consciences, and hearts, and minds! So Milton, fabling, sings of angels fallen from their first estate, seeking to enter Pandemonium: —

"They but now who seemed
In bigness to surpass Earth's giant-sons,
Now less than smallest dwarfs, in narrow room
Throng numberless, ...
. . . . to smallest forms
Reduced their shapes immense, and were at large,
Though without number still, amidst the hall
Of that infernal court."

Mr. Webster stamped his foot, and broke through into the great hollow of practical atheism, which undergulfs the state and church. Then what a caving in was there! The firm-set base of northern cities quaked and yawned with gaping rents. "Penn's sandy foundation" shook again, and black men fled from the city of brotherly love, as doves flee from a farmer's barn when summer lightning stabs the roof. There was a twist in Faneuil Hall, and the doors could not open wide enough for Liberty to regain her ancient Cradle; only soldiers, greedy to steal a man, themselves stole out and in. Ecclesiastic quicksand ran down the hole amain. Metropolitan churches toppled, and pitched, and canted, and cracked, their bowing walls all out of plumb. Colleges, broken from the chain which held them in the stream of time, rushed towards the abysmal rent. Harvard led the way, *Christo et Ecclesiæ* in its hand. Down plunged Andover, "Conscience and the Constitution" clutched in its ancient, failing arm. New Haven began to cave in. Doctors of Divinity, orthodox, heterodox with only a doxy of doubt, "no settled opinion," had great alacrity in sinking, and went down quick, as live as ever, into the pit of Korah, Dathan, and Abiram, the bottomless pit of lower law, — one with his mother, cloaked by a surplice, hid neath his sinister arm, and an acknowledged brother grasped by his remaining limb. Fossils of theology, dead as Ezekiel's bones, took to their feet again, and stood up for most arrant wrong. "There is no higher law of God," quoth they, as they went down; "no golden rule, only the statutes of men." A man with mythologic ear might fancy that he heard a snickering laugh run round the world below, snorting, whinnying, and neighing, as it echoed from the infernal spot pressed by the fallen monsters of ill-fame, who, thousands of years ago, on the same errand, plunged down the self-same way. What tidings the echo bore, Dante nor Milton could not tell. Let us leave that to darkness, and to silence, and to death.

But spite of all this, in every city, in every town, in every college, and in each capsizing church, there were found faithful men, who feared not the monster, heeded not the stamping, — nay, Doctors of Divinity were found living, — in all their houses there was light, and the destroying angel shook them not. The word of the Lord came in open vision to their eye; they had their lamps trimmed and burning, their loins girt; they stood road-ready. Liberty and Religion turned in thither, and the slave found bread and wings. "When my father and my mother forsake me, then the Lord will hold me up!"

After the 7th of March, Mr. Webster became the ally of the worst of men, the forefront of kidnapping. The orator of Plymouth Rock was the advocate of slavery; the hero of Bunker Hill put chains around Boston Court-house; the applauder of Adams and Jefferson was a tool of the slaveholder, and a keeper of slavery's dogs, the associate of the kidnapper, and the mocker of men who loved the right. Two years he lived with that rabble rout for company, his name the boast of every vilest thing. "Oh, how unlike the place from whence he fell!" In early life, Mr. Hill, of New Hampshire, pursued him with unrelenting bitterness. Of late years Mr. Webster had complained of this, declaring that "Mr. Hill had done more than any other man to debauch the character of New Hampshire, bringing the bitterness of politics into private life." After that day of St. Judas, Mr. Webster pursued the same course which Mr. Hill had followed forty years before, and the two enemies were reconciled.* The Herod of the Democrats and the Pilate of Federalism were made friends by the Fugitive Slave Bill, and rode in the same "Omnibus,"— "a blue-light Federalist" and "a genuine Democrat dyed in the wool."

Think of him! — the Daniel Webster of Plymouth Rock

* See Letter of Hon. Isaac Hill (April 17, 1850), and Mr. Webster's Reply.

advocating the Compromise Measures! the Daniel Webster of Faneuil Hall, who spoke with the inspiration of Samuel Adams and the tongue of James Otis, honoring the holy dead with his praise! — think of him at Buffalo, Albany, Syracuse, scoffing at modern men, who "perilled their lives, their fortunes, and their sacred honor," to visit the fatherless and the widows in their affliction, and to keep themselves unspotted from the world! — think of him threatening with the gallows such as clothed the naked, fed the hungry, visited the prisoner, and gave a cup of cold water to him that was ready to perish! Think of Daniel Webster become the assassin of Liberty in the Capitol! Think of him, full of the Old Testament and dear Isaac Watts, scoffing at the higher law of God, while the mountains of Virginia looked him in the face!

But what was the recompense? Ask Massachusetts, — ask the North. Let the Baltimore Convention tell. He was the greatest candidate before it. General Scott is a little man when the feathers are gone. Fillmore, you know him. Both of these, for greatness of intellect, compared to Webster, were as a single magpie measured by an eagle. Look at his speeches; look at his forehead; look at his face! The two hundred and ninety-three delegates came together and voted. They gave him thirty-three votes, and that only once! Where were the men of the "lower law," who made denial of God the first principle of their politics? Where were they who in Faneuil Hall scoffed and jeered at the "higher law;" or at Capron Springs, who "laughed" when he mocked at the law higher than the Virginia hills? Where were the kidnappers?

The "lower law" men and the kidnappers strained themselves to the utmost, and he had thirty-three votes.

Where was the South? Fifty-three times did the Convention ballot, and the South never gave him a vote, — not a vote; no, not one! Northern friends — I honor their affection for the great man — went to the South, and begged for the poor and paltry pittance of a seeming vote, in order to break the bitterness of the fall! They went "with tears in their eyes," and in mercy's name, and asked that crumb from the Southern board. But the cruel South, treacherous to him whom she beguiled to treason against God, she answered, "Not a vote!" It was the old fate of men who betray. Southern politicians "did not dare dispense with the services thrust on him, but revenged themselves by withdrawing his well-merited reward." It was the fate of Strafford, the fate of Wolsey. When Lasthenes and Euthycrates betrayed Olynthus to Macedonian Philip, fighting against the liberties of Greece, they were distinguished — if Demosthenes be right — only by the cruelty of their fate. Mr. Webster himself had a forefeeling that it might be so; for, on the morning of his fatal speech, he told a brother Senator, "I have my doubts that the speech I am going to make will ruin me." But he played the card with a heavy, a rash, and not a skilful hand. It was only the playing of a card, — his last card. Mr. Calhoun had said, "The farthest Southerner is nearer to us than the nearest Northern man." They could trust him with their work, — not with its covenanted pay!

Oh! Cardinal Wolsey! there was never such a fall. "He fell, like Lucifer, never to hope again!" The telegraph which brought him tidings of his fate was a thunderstroke out of the clear sky. No wonder that he wept, and said, "I am a disgraced man, a ruined man!" His early, his last, his fondest dream of ambition broke, and only ruin filled his hand! What a spectacle to move pity in the stones of the street!

But it seemed as if nothing could be spared him. His cup of bitterness, already full, was made to run over; for joyous men, full of wine and the nomination, called him up at midnight out of his bed — the poor, disappointed old man! — to "congratulate him on the nomination of Scott!" And they forced the great man, falling back on his self-respect, to say that the next morning he should "rise with the lark, as jocund and as gay."

Was not that enough? Oh, there is no pity in the hearts of men! Even that was not enough! Northern friends went to him, and asked him to advise men to vote for Gen. Scott!

Gen. Scott is said to be an anti-slavery man; but soon as the political carpenters put the "planks" together at Baltimore, he scrambled upon the platform, and stands there on all-fours to this day, looking for "fellow-citizens, native and adopted," listening for "that brogue," and declaring that, after all, he is "only a common man." Did you ever read Gen. Scott's speeches? Then think of asking Daniel Webster to recommend him for President, — Scott in the chair, and Webster out! That was gall after the wormwood! They say that Daniel Webster did write a letter advocating the election of Scott, and afterwards said, "I still live." If he did so, attribute it to the wanderings of a great mind, shattered by sickness; and be assured he would have taken it back, if he had ever set his firm foot on the ground again!

Daniel Webster went down to Marshfield — to die! He died of his 7th of March speech! That word endorsed on Mason's Bill drove thousands of fugitives from America to Canada. It put chains round our court-house; it led men to violate the majesty of law all over the North. I violated it, and so did you. It sent Thomas Sims in fetters to his jail and his scourging at Savannah; it caused practical atheism to be preached in many churches of New York, Philadelphia, Washington, and, worst of all, Boston itself! and then, with its own recoil, it sent Daniel Webster to his grave, giving him such a reputation as a man would not wish for his utterest foe.

No event in the American Revolution was half so terrible as his speeches in defence of slavery and kidnapping, his abrogation of the right to discuss all measures of the government. We lost battles again and again, lost campaigns — our honor we never lost. The army was without powder at Cambridge, in '76; without shoes and blankets in '78; and the bare feet of New England valor marked the ice with blood when they crossed the Delaware. But we were never without conscience, never without morality. Powder might fail, and shoes drop, old and rotten, from soldiers' feet. But the love of God was in the American heart, and no American general said, "There is no law higher than the Blue Ridge!" Nay, they appealed to God's higher law, not thinking that in politics religion makes men mad.

While the Philip of slavery was thundering at our gate, the American Demosthenes advised us to "conquer our prejudices" against letting him in; to throw down the wall "with alacrity," and bid him come: it was a constitutional Philip. How silver dims the edge of steel! When the tongue of freedom was cut out of the mouth of Europe by the sabres of tyrants, and only in the British Isles and in Saxon speech could liberty be said or sung, the greatest orator who ever spoke the language of Milton and Burke told us to suppress discussion! In the dark and troubled night of American politics, our tallest Pharo on the shore hung out a false beacon.

Said Mr. Webster once, "There will always be some perverse minds who will vote the wrong way, let the justice of the case be ever so apparent."* Did he know what he was doing? Too well. In the winter of 1850, he partially prepared a speech in defence of freedom. Was his own amendment to Mason's Bill designed to be its text?† Some say so. I know not. He wrote to an intimate and

* "Columbian Centinel," March 11, 1820.

† Works, vol. v. p. 373–4.

sagacious friend in Boston, asking, How far can I go in defence of freedom, and have Massachusetts sustain me? The friend repaid the confidence and said, Far as you like! Mr. Webster went as far as New Orleans, as far as Texas and the Del Norte, in support of slavery! When that speech came, — the rawest wind of March, — the friend declared: It seldom happens to any man to be able to disgrace the generation he is born in. But the opportunity has presented itself to Mr. Webster, and he has done the deed!

Cardinal Wolsey fell, and lost nothing but his place. Bacon fell; the "wisest, brightest," lived long enough to prove himself the "meanest of mankind." Strafford came down. But it was nothing to the fall of Webster. The Anglo-Saxon race never knew such a terrible and calamitous ruin. His downfall shook the continent. Truth fell prostrate in the street. Since then, the court-house has a twist in its walls, and equity cannot enter its door; the steeples point awry, and the "higher law" is hurled down from the pulpit. One priest would enslave all the "posterity of Ham," and another would drive a fugitive from his own door; a third is certain that Paul was a kidnapper; and a fourth has the assurance of his consciousness that Christ Jesus would have sold and bought slaves. Practical atheism became common in the pulpits of America; they forgot that there was a God. In the hard winter of 1780, if Fayette had copied Arnold, and Washington gone over to the enemy, the fall could not have been worse. Benedict Arnold fell, but fell through, — so low that no man quotes him for precedent. Aaron Burr is only a warning. Webster fell, and he lay there "not less than archangel ruined," and enticed the nation in his fall. Shame on us! — all those three are of New England blood!

My friends, it is hard for me to say these things. My

mother's love is warm in my own bosom still, and I hate to say these words. But God is just; and, in the presence of God, I stand here to tell the truth.

Did men honor Daniel Webster? So did I. I was a boy ten years old when he stood at Plymouth Rock, and never shall I forget how his clarion-words rang in my boyish heart. I was but a little boy when he spoke those brave words in behalf of Greece. I learned to hate slavery from the lips of that great intellect; and now that he takes back his word, and comes himself to be Slavery's slave, I hate it ten-fold harder than before, because it made a bondman out of that proud, powerful nature.

Did men love him? So did I. Not blindly, but as I loved a great mind, as the defender of the Constitution and the unalienable rights of man.

Sober and religious men of Boston yet mourn that their brothers were kidnapped in the city of Hancock and Adams — it was Daniel Webster who kidnapped them. Massachusetts has wept at the deep iniquity which was wrought in her capital — it was done by the man whom she welcomed to her bosom, and long had loved to honor. Let history, as

> "Sad as angels at the good man's sin,
> Blush to record, and weep to give it in!"

Do men mourn for him? See how they mourn! The streets are hung with black. The newspapers are sad colored. The shops are put in mourning. The Mayor and Aldermen wear crape. Wherever his death is made known, the public business stops, and flags drop half-mast down. The courts adjourn. The courts of Massachusetts — at Boston, at Dedham, at Lowell, all adjourn; the courts of New Hampshire, of Maine, of New York; even at Baltimore and Washington, the courts adjourn; for the great lawyer is dead, and Justice must wait another day. Only the United States Court, in Boston, trying a man for helping

Shadrach out of the furnace of the kidnappers, — the court that executes the Fugitive Slave Law, — that does not adjourn; that keeps on; its worm dies not, and the fire of its persecution is not quenched, when death puts out the lamp of life. Injustice is hungry for its prey, and must not be balked. It was very proper! Symbolical court of the Fugitive Slave Bill — it does not respect life, why should it death? and, scorning liberty, why should it heed decorum? Did the judges deem that Webster's spirit, on its way to God, would look at Plymouth Rock, then pause on the spots made more classic by his eloquence, and gaze at Bunker Hill, and tarry his hour in the august company of noble men at Faneuil Hall, and be glad to know that injustice was chanting his requiem in that court? They greatly misjudge the man. I know Daniel Webster better, and I appeal for him against his idly judging friends.*

Do men now mourn for him, the great man eloquent? I put on sackcloth long ago; I mourned for him when he wrote the Creole letter, which surprised Ashburton, Briton that he was. I mourned when he spoke the speech of the 7th of March. I mourned when the Fugitive Slave Bill passed Congress, and the same cannons which have fired minute-guns for him fired also one hundred rounds of joy for the forging of a new fetter for the fugitive's foot. I mourned for him when the kidnappers first came to Boston, — hated then, now "respectable men," "the companions of princes," enlarging their testimony in the court. I mourned when my own parishioners fled from the "stripes" of New England to the "stars" of Old England. I mourned when Ellen Craft fled to my house for shelter and for succor, and for the first

* I am told that there was some technical reason why that court continued its session. I know nothing of the motive; but I believe it was the fact that the only court in the United States which did not adjourn at the intelligence of the death of Mr. Webster, was the court which was seeking to punish a man for rescuing *Shadrach* from the fiery furnace made ready for him.

time in all my life I armed this hand. I mourned when I married William and Ellen Craft, and gave them a Bible for their soul, and a sword to keep that soul living in a living frame. I mourned when the court-house was hung in chains; when Thomas Sims, from his dungeon, sent out his petition for prayers, and the churches did not dare to pray. I mourned when that poor outcast in yonder dungeon sent for me to visit him, and when I took him by the hand which Daniel Webster was chaining in that hour. I mourned for Webster when we prayed our prayer and sang our psalm on Long Wharf in the morning's gray. I mourned then: I shall not cease to mourn. The flags will be removed from the streets, the cannon will sound their other notes of joy; but, for me, I shall go mourning all my days; I shall refuse to be comforted; and at last I shall lay down my gray hairs with weeping and with sorrow in the grave. O Webster! Webster! would God that I had died for thee!

He was a powerful man physically, a man of a large mould, — a great body and a great brain: he seemed made to last a hundred years. Since Socrates, there has seldom been a head so massive huge, save the stormy features of Michael Angelo, —

"The hand that rounded Peter's dome,
And groined the aisles of Christian Rome;"

he who sculptured Day and Night into such beautiful forms, — looked them in his face before he chiselled them in stone. The cubic capacity of his head surpassed all former measurements of mind. Since Charlemagne, I think there has not been such a grand figure in all Christendom. A large man, decorous in dress, dignified in deportment, he walked as if he felt himself a king. Men from the country, who knew him not, stared at him as he passed through our streets. The coal-heavers and porters of London looked on him as one of the great forces of the globe: they recognized a native king. In the Senate of the United States, he looked an emperor in that council. Even the majestic Calhoun seemed common compared with him. Clay looked vulgar, and Van Buren but a fox. His countenance, like Strafford's, was "manly black." His mind —

> "Was lodged in a fair and lofty room.
> On his brow
> Sat terror, mixed with wisdom; and, at once,
> Saturn and Hermes in his countenance."

What a mouth he had! It was a lion's mouth; yet there was a sweet grandeur in his smile, and a woman's softness when he would. What a brow it was! what eyes! like charcoal fires in the bottom of a deep, dark well. His face was rugged with volcanic fires, — great passions and great thoughts.

> "The front of Jove himself;
> An eye like Mars to threaten and command."

Let me examine the elements of Mr. Webster's character in some detail. Divide the faculties, not bodily, into intellectual, moral, affectional, and religious, and see what he had of each, beginning with the highest.

I. His latter life shows that he had no large development of the religious powers, which join men consciously to the infinite God. He had little religion in the higher meaning of that word, much in the lower. He had the conventional form of religion, — the formality of outward and visible prayer; reverence for the Bible and the name of Christ; attendance at meeting on Sundays and at the "ordinances of religion." He was a "devout man," in the ecclesiastic sense of the word. But it is easy to be devout, hard to be moral. Of the two men, in the parable, who "went up to the temple to pray," only the Pharisee was "devout" in the common sense. Devoutness took the Priest and the

Levite to the temple: morality took the good Samaritan to the man fallen among thieves.

His reputation for religion seems to rest on these facts,— that he read the Bible, and knew more passages from it than most political editors, more than some clergymen; he thought Job "a great epic poem," and quoted Habbakuk by rote;—that he knew many hymns by heart; attended what is called "divine service;" agreed with a New Hampshire divine "in all the doctrines of a Christian life;" and, in the "Girard case," praised the popular theology, with the ministers thereof,—the latter as "appointed by the Author of the Christian religion himself."

He seems by nature to have had a religious turn of mind; was full of devout and reverential feelings; took a deep delight in religious emotions; was fond of religious books of a sentimental cast; loved Watts's tender and delicious hymns, with the devotional parts of the Bible; his memory was stored with the poetry of hymn-books; he was fond of attendance at church. He had no particle of religious bigotry; joining an Orthodox Church at Boscawen, an Episcopal at Washington, a Unitarian at Boston, and attending religious services without much regard for the theology of the minister. He loved religious forms, and could not see a child baptized without dropping a tear. Psalms and hymns also brought the woman into those great eyes. He was never known to swear, or use any profanity of speech. Considering the habits of his political company, that is a fact worth notice. But I do not find that his religious emotions had any influence on his latter life, either public or private. He read religion out of politics with haughty scorn,—"It makes men mad"! It appeared neither to check him from ill, nor urge to good: though he loved "to have religion made a personal matter," he forsook the church which made it personal in the form of temperance. His "religious character" was what the churches tend to form, and love to praise.

II. Of the affections he was well provided by nature, though they were little cultivated,—attachable to a few who knew him, and loved him tenderly; and, if he hated like a giant, he loved also like a king.

He had small respect for the mass of men,—a contempt for the judgment and the feelings of the millions who make up the people. Many women loved him; some from pure affection, others fascinated and overborne by the immense masculineness of the man. Some are still left who knew him in early life, before political ambition set its mark on his forehead, and drove him forth into the world: they love him with the tenderest of woman's affection. This is no small praise. In his earlier life he was fond of children, loved their prattle and their play. They, too, were fond of him, came to him as dust of iron to a loadstone, climbed on his back, or, when he lay down, lay on his limbs and also slept.

Of unimpassioned and unrelated love, there are two modes,—friendship for a few; philanthropy for all. Friendship he surely had, especially in earlier life. All along the shore, men loved him; men in Boston loved him to the last; Washington held loving hearts which worshipped him. But, of late years, he turned round to smite and crush his early friends who kept the higher law; ambition tore the friendship out of him, and he became unkind and cruel. The companions of his later years were chiefly low men, with large animal appetites, servants of his body's baser parts, or tide-waiters of his ambition,—vulgar men in Boston and New York, who bask in the habitations of cruelty, whereof the dark places of the earth are full, seeking to enslave their brother-men. These barnacles clove to the great man's unprotected parts, and hastened his decay. When kidnappers made their loathsome lair of his bosom, what was his friendship worth?

Of philanthropy, I claim not much for him. The noble plea for Greece is the most I can put in for argument. He cared little for the poor; charity seldom invaded his open purse; he trod down the poorest and most friendless of perishing men. His name was never connected with the humanities of the age. Soon as the American Government seemed fixed on the side of cruelty, he marched all his dreadful artillery over, and levelled his breaching cannons against men ready to perish without his shot. In later years, his face was the visage of a tyrant.

III. Of conscience it seemed to me he had little; in his later life, exceeding little: his moral sense seemed long besotted; almost, though not wholly, gone. Hence, though he was often generous, he was not just. Free to give as to grasp, he was lavish by instinct, not charitable on principle.

He had little courage, and rarely spoke a Northern word to a Southern audience, save his official words in Congress. In Charleston he was the "schoolmaster that gives us no lessons." He quailed before the Southern men who would "dissolve the Union," when he stood before their eye. They were "high-minded and chivalrous:" it was only the non-resistants of the North he meant to ban!

He was indeed eminently selfish, joining the instinctive egotism of passion with the self-conscious, voluntary, deliberate, calculating egotism of ambition. He borrowed money of rich young men — ay, and of poor ones — in the generosity of their youth, and never paid. He sought to make his colleagues in office the tools of his ambition, and, that failing, pursued them with the intensest hate. Thus he sought to ruin the venerable John Quincy Adams, when the President became a Representative. By secret hands he scattered circulars in Mr. Adams's district to work his overthrow; got other men to oppose him. With different men he succeeded better. He used his party as he used his friends, — as tools. He coquetted with the Democrats in '42, with the Free Soilers in '48; but, the suit miscarrying, turned to the Slave Power in '50, and negotiated an espousal which was cruelly broke off in '52. Men, parties, the law,* and the nation, he did not hesitate to sacrifice to the colossal selfishness of his egotistic ambition.

His strength lay not in the religious, nor in the affectional, nor in the moral part of man.

IV. But his intellect was immense. His power of comprehension was vast. He methodized swiftly. If you look at the forms of intellectual action, you may distribute them into three great modes; the Understanding, the Imagination, and the Reason; — the Understanding dealing with details and methods, the practical power; Imagination, with beauty, the power to create; Reason, with first principles and universal laws, the philosophic power.

We must deny to Mr. Webster the great Reason. He does not belong at all to the chief men of that department, — with Socrates, Aristotle, Plato, Leibnitz, Newton, Des Cartes, and the other mighties. Nay, he has no place with humbler men of reason, with common philosophers; he had no philosophical system of politics, few philosophical ideas of politics, whereof to make a system. He seldom grasps a universal law. His measures of expediency for to-day are seldom bottomed on universal principles of right, which last for ever.

I cannot assign to him large Imagination. He was not creative of new forms of thought or of beauty; so he lacks the poetic charm which gladdens the loftiest eloquence.

But his Understanding was exceedingly great. He acquired readily and retained well; arranged with ease and skill, and fluently reproduced. As a scholar, he passed for learned in the American Senate, where scholars are few; for a universal man, with editors of political and commercial prints. But his learning was narrow in its range, and not very nice in its accuracy. His reach in history and literature was very small for a man seventy years of age, always

* Leges invalidæ prius; imo nocere coactæ.

associating with able men. To science he seems to have paid scarce any attention at all. It is a short radius that measures the arc of his historic realm. A few Latin authors, whom he loved to quote, made up his meagre classic store. He was not a scholar, and it is idle to claim great scholarship for him. Compare him with the prominent statesmen of Europe, or with the popular orators of England, you see continually the narrow range of his culture.

As a statesman, his lack of what I call the higher Reason and Imagination continually appears. He invented nothing. To the national stock he added no new idea, created out of new thought; no new maxim, formed by induction out of human history and old thought. The great ideas of the time were not borne in his bosom.

He organized nothing. There were great ideas of immense practical value seeking lodgment in a body: he aided them not. None of the great measures of our time were his — not one of them. His best bill was the Specie Bill of 1815, which caused payments to be made in national currency.

His lack of conscience is painfully evident. As Secretary of State, he did not administer eminently well. When Secretary of State under Mr. Tyler, he knew how to be unjust to poor, maltreated Mexico. His letters in reply to the just complaints of Mr. Bocanegra, the Mexican Secretary of State, are painful to read: it is the old story of the Wolf and the Lamb.*

The appointments made under his administration had better not be looked at too closely. The affairs of Cuba last year and this, the affairs of the Fisheries and the Lobos Islands, are little to his credit.

* See these letters — to Mr. Thompson, Works, vol. vi. p. 445, *et seq.*; and those of Mr. Bocanegra to Mr. Webster, p. 442, *et seq.* 457, *et seq.* How different is the tone of America to powerful England! Whom men wrong they hate.

He was sometimes ignorant of the affairs he had to treat; he neglected the public business, — left grave matters all unattended to. Nay, he did worse. Early in August last, Mr. Lawrence had an interview with the British Foreign Secretary, in which explanations were made calculated to remove all anxiety as to the Fishery Question. He wrote a paper detailing the result of the interview. It was designed to be communicated to the American Senate. Mr. Lawrence sent it to Mr. Webster. It reached the Department at Washington on the 24th of August. But Mr. Webster did not communicate it to the Senate; even the President knew nothing of its existence till after the Secretary's death. Now, it is not "compatible with the public interest to publish it," as its production would reveal the negligence of the Department. You remember the letter he published on his own account relating to the Fisheries! No man, it was said, could get office under his administration, "unless bathed in negro's blood:" support of the Fugitive Slave Bill, "like the path of righteous devotion, led to a blessed preferment."

Lacking both moral principle and intellectual ideas, political ethics and political economy, it must needs be that his course in politics was crooked. He opposed the Mexican war, but invested a son in it, and praised the soldiers who fought in it, as surpassing our fathers who stood behind bulwarks on Bunker Hill! He called on the nation to uphold the stars of America on the fields of Mexico, though he knew it was the stripes that they held up. Now, he is for free trade, then for protection; now for specie, then for bills; first for a bank, then it is "an obsolete idea;" now for freedom and against slavery, then for slavery and against freedom; now Justice is the object of government, now Money. Now what makes men Christians makes them good citizens; next, religion is good "everywhere but in politics, — there it makes men mad." Now religion is the only ground of government, and all conscience is to be respected; next, there is no law higher than the act of Congress, and he hoots at conscience, and would not re-enact the law of God.

He began his career as the friend of free trade and hard money; he would restrict the government to the strait line of the Constitution rigidly defined; he would resist the Bank, the protective tariff, the extension of slavery, they exceeded the limits of the Constitution; he became the pensioned advocate of restricted trade and of paper money; he interpreted the Constitution to oppress the several States and the citizens; brought the force of the government against private right, and lent all his might to the extension of slavery. Once he stood out boldly for the right of all men "to canvass public measures and the merits of public men;" then he tells us that discussion "must be suppressed"! Several years ago, he called a private meeting of the principal manufacturers of Boston, and advised them to abandon the protective tariff; but they would not, and so he defended it as warmly as ever! His course was crooked as the Missouri. The Duke of Wellington and Sir Robert Peel were, like him, without a philosophical scheme of political conduct, or any great ideas whereby to shape the future into fairer forms; but the principle of duty was the thread which joined all parts of their public ministration. Thereon each strung his victories. But selfish egotism is the only continuous thread I find thus running through the crooked life of the famous American.

With such a lack of ideas and of honesty, with a dread of taking the responsibility in advance of public opinion, lacking confidence in the people, and confidence in himself, he did not readily understand the public opinion on which he depended. He thought himself "a favorite with the people," — "sure of election if nominated;" it was "only the politicians" who stood between him and the nation. He thought the Fugitive Slave Bill would be popular in the North; that it could be executed in Syracuse, and Massachusetts would conquer her prejudices with alacrity. So he had little value as a permanent guide: he changed often, but at the unlucky moment.

He tacked and wore ship many a time in his life, always in bad weather, and never came round but he fell off from the popular wind. Perseverance makes the saints: he always forsook his idea just as that was about to make its fortune. In his voyaging for the Presidency, he was always too late for the tide; embarked on the ebb, and was left as the stream run dry. The Fugitive Slave Law has done the South no good, save to reveal the secrets of her prison-house, the cabin of Uncle Tom, and make the North hate slavery with a tenfold hate. So far as he "Websterized" the Whig party, he has done so to its ruin.

He was a great advocate, a great orator; it is said, the greatest in the land,—and I do not doubt that this was true. Surely he was immensely great. When he spoke, he was a grand spectacle. His noble form, so dignified and masculine; his massive head; the mighty brow, Olympian in its majesty; the great, deep, dark eye, which, like a lion's, seemed fixed on objects far off, looking beyond what lay in easy range; the mouth so full of strength and determination,—these all became the instruments of such eloquence as few men ever hear. He magnetized men by his presence; he subdued them by his will more than by his argument. Many have surpassed him in written words; for he could not embody the sunshine in such flowers of thought as Burke, Milton, and Cicero wrought into mosaic oratory. But, since the great Athenians, Demosthenes and Pericles, who ever thundered out such spoken eloquence as he?

Yet he has left no perfect specimen of a great oration. He had not the instinctive genius which creates a beautiful whole by nature, as a mother bears a living son; nor the wide knowledge, the deep philosophy, the plastic industry, which forms a beautiful whole by art, as a sculptor chisels a marble boy. So his greatest and most deliberate efforts of oratory will not bear comparison with the great eloquence of nature that is born, nor the great eloquence of art that is made. Compared therewith, his mighty works are as Hercules compared with Apollo. It is an old world, and excellence in oratory is difficult; yet he has sentences and paragraphs that I think unsurpassed and unequalled, and I do not see how they can ever fade. He was not a Nile of eloquence, cascading into poetic beauty now, then watering whole provinces with the drainage of tropic mountains: he was a Niagara, pouring a world of clear waters adown a single ledge.

His style was simple, the business-style of a strong man. Now and then it swelled into beauty, though it was often dull. In later years, he seldom touched the conscience, the affections, or the soul, except, alas! to smite our sense of justice, our philanthropy, and trust in God. He always addressed the understanding, not the reason, — Calhoun did that the more, — not the imagination: in his speech there was little wit, little beauty, little poetry. He laid siege to the understanding. Here lay his strength — he could make a statement better than any man in America; had immense power of argumentation, building a causeway from his will to the hearer's mind. He was skilful in devising "middle terms," in making steps whereby to lead the audience to his determination. No man managed the elements of his argument with more practical effect.

Perhaps he did this better when contending for a wrong, than when battling for the right. His most ingenious arguments are pleas for injustice.* Part of the effect came from the physical bulk of the man; part from the bulk of will,

* See examples of this in the Creole letter, and that to Mr. Thompson (Works, vol. vi.), and in many a speech.

which marked all his speech, and writing too; but much from his power of statement. He gathered a great mass of material, bound it together, swung it about his head, fixed his eye on the mark, then let the ruin fly. If you want a word suddenly shot from Dover to Calais, you send it by lightning; if a ball of a ton weight, you get a steam-cannon to pitch it across. Webster was the steam-gun of eloquence. He hit the mark less by gunnery than strength. His shot seemed big as his target.*

There is a great difference in the weapons which speakers use. This orator brings down his quarry with a single subtle shot, of sixty to the pound. He carries death without weight in his gun, as sure as fate.

Here is another, the tin-pedlar of American speech. He is a snake in the grass, slippery, shining, with a baleful crest on his head, cunning in his crazy eye, and the poison of the old serpent in his heart, and on his slimy jaw, and about the fang at the bottom of his smooth and forked and nimble tongue. He conquers by bewitching; he fascinates his game to death.

Commonly, Mr. Webster was open and honest in his oratory. He had no masked batteries, no Quaker guns. He had "that rapid and vehement declamation which fixes the hearer's attention on the subject, making the speaker forgotten, and leaving his art concealed." He wheeled his forces into line, column after column, with the quickness of Hannibal and the masterly arrangement of Cæsar, and, like Napoleon, broke the centre of his opponent's line by the superior weight of his own column and the sudden heaviness of his fire. Thus he laid siege to the understanding, and carried it by dint of cannonade. This was his strategy,

* "Tu quoque, Piso,
Judicis affectum, possessaque pectora ducis
Victor; sponte sua sequitur, quocunque vocasti:
Et te dante capit judex, quam non habet iram."

in the court-house, in the senate, and in the public hall. There were no ambuscades, no pitfalls, or treacherous Indian subtlety. It was the tactics of a great and naturally honest-minded man.

In his oratory there was but one trick, — the trick of self-depreciation. That came on him in his later years, and it always failed. He was too big to make any one believe he thought himself little; so obviously proud, we knew he valued his services high when he rated them so low. That comprehensive eye could not overlook so great an object as himself. He was not organized to cheat, to deceive; and did not prosper when he tried. 'Tis ill the lion apes the fox.

He was ambitious. Cardinal Wolsey's "unbounded stomach" was also the stomach of Webster. Yet his ambition mostly failed. In forty years of public life, he rose no higher than Secretary of State; and held that post but five years. He was continually out-generalled by subtler men. He had little political foresight: for he had not the all-conquering Religion which meekly executes the Law of God, all fearless of its consequence; nor yet the wide Philanthropy, the deep sympathy with all that is human, which gives a man the public heart, and so the control of the issues of life, which thence proceed; nor the great Justice which sees the everlasting right, and journeys thitherward through good or ill; nor the mighty Reason, which, reflecting, beholds the principles of human nature, the constant mode of operation of the forces of God in the forms of men; nor the poetic Imagination, which in its political sphere creates great schemes of law; and hence he was not popular.

He longed for the Presidency; but Harrison kept him from the nomination in '40, Clay in '44, Taylor in '48, and Scott in '52. He never had a wide and original influence in the politics of the nation; for he had no elemental thunder of his own — the Tariff was Mr. Calhoun's at first; the Force Bill was from another hand; the Fugitive Slave Bill was Mr. Mason's; "the Omnibus" had many fathers, whereof Webster was not one. He was not a blood-relation to any of the great measures, — to free-trade or protection, to paper money or hard coin, to freedom or slavery; he was of their kindred only by adoption. He has been on all sides of most questions, save on the winning side.

In the case of the Fugitive Slave Law, he stood betwixt the living and the dead, and blessed the plague. But, even here, he faltered when he came North again, — "The South will get no concessions from me." Mr. Webster commended the first draught of the Fugitive Slave Bill, with Mr. Mason's amendments thereto, volunteering his support thereof "to the fullest extent." But he afterwards and repeatedly declared, "The Fugitive Slave Bill was not such a measure as I had prepared before I left the Senate, and which I should have supported if I had remained in the Senate."* "I was of opinion," said he, "that a summary trial by jury might be had, which would satisfy the prejudices of the people, and produce no harm to those who claimed the services of fugitives."† Nay, he went so far as to introduce a bill to the Senate providing a trial by jury for all fugitives claiming a trial for their freedom.‡ He thought the whole business of delivering up such as owed service or labor, belonged to the State whither the fugitive fled, and not to the general government.§ Of course he must have considered it constitutional and expedient to secure for the fugitive a trial before an impartial jury of "twelve good and lawful men," who should pass upon the

* Mr. Webster's letter to the Union Committee. Works, vol. vi. p. 578, *et al.*

† Speech at Syracuse (New York, 1851), p. 17.

‡ See it in Works, vol. v. p. 373–4.

§ *Ibid.* p. 354.

whole matter at issue. But, with that conviction, and with that bill ready drafted, as he says, in his desk, he could volunteer his support to a bill which took away from the States all jurisdiction in the matter, and from the fugitive all "due process of law," all trial by jury, and left him in the hands of a creature of the court, who was to be paid twice as much for enslaving his victim as for acquitting a man! He had almost no self-reliant independence of character. It was his surroundings, not his will, that shaped his course, — "driven by the wind and tossed."

Mr. Webster's political career began with generous promise. He contended for the rights of the people against the government, of the minority against the majority; he defended the right of each man to discuss all public measures, and the conduct of public men; he wished commerce to be unrestricted, payments to be made in hard coin. He spoke noble words against oppression, — the despotism of the "Holy Alliance" in Europe, the cruelty of the Slave Trade in America. Generously and nobly he contended against the extension of slavery beyond the Mississippi. Not philanthropic by instinct or moral principle, averse to democratic institutions both by nature and conviction, he yet, by instinctive generosity, hated tyranny, hated injustice, hated despotism. He appealed to moral power against physical force. He sympathized with the republics of South America. His great powers taking such a direction certainly promised a brilliant future, large services for mankind. But, alas! he fell on evil times: who ever fell on any other? He was intensely ambitious; not ambitious to serve mankind, but to hold office, have power and fame. Is this the "last infirmity of noble mind"? It was not a very noble object he proposed as the end of his life; the means to it became successively more and more unworthy. "Ye cannot serve God and mammon."

For some years, no large body of men has had much

trust in him, — admiration, but not confidence. In Massachusetts, off the pavements, for the last three years, he has had but little power. After the speech of March 7, he said, "I WILL be maintained in Massachusetts." Massachusetts said No! Only in the cities that bought him was he omnipotent. Even the South would not trust him. Gen. Jackson was the most popular man of our time. Calhoun was popular throughout the South; Clay, in all quarters of the land; and, at this day, Seward wields the forces of the Whigs. With all his talent, Webster never had the influence on America of the least of these.

Yet Daniel Webster had many popular qualities. He loved out-door and manly sports, — boating, fishing, fowling. He was fond of nature, loving New Hampshire's mountain scenery. He had started small and poor, had risen great and high, and honorably had fought his way alone. He rose early in the morning. He loved gardening, "the purest of human pleasures." He was a farmer, and took a countryman's delight in country things, — in loads of hay, in trees, in turnips and the noble Indian corn, in monstrous swine. He had a patriarch's love of sheep, — choice breeds thereof he had. He took delight in cows, — short horned Durhams, Herefordshires, Ayrshires, Alderneys. He tilled paternal acres with his own oxen. He loved to give the kine fodder. It was pleasant to hear his talk of oxen. And but three days before he left the earth, too ill to visit them, his cattle, lowing, came to see their sick lord; and, as he stood in his door, his great oxen were driven up, that he might smell their healthy breath, and look his last on those broad, generous faces, that were never false to him.

He loved birds, and would not have them shot on his premises; and so his farm twittered all over with their "sweet jargonings." Though in public his dress was more uniformly new than is common with acknowledged gentlemen, at home and on his estate he wore his old and homely clothes, and had kind words for all, and hospitality besides. He loved his father and brother with great tenderness, which easily broke into tears when he spoke of them. He was kind to his obscurer and poor relations. He had no money to bestow; they could not share his intellect, or the renown it gave. But he gave them his affection, and they loved him with veneration. He was a friendly man: all along the shore there were plain men that loved him, — whom he also loved; "a good neighbor, a good townsman:"

> "Lofty and sour to those that loved him not;
> But to those men that sought him, sweet as summer."

His influence on the development of America has not been great. He had large gifts, large opportunities also for their use, — the two greatest things which great men ask. Yet he has brought little to pass. No great ideas, no great organizations, will bind him to the coming age. His life has been a long vacillation. Ere long, men will ask for the historic proof to verify the reputation of his power. It will not appear. For the present, his career is a failure: he was balked of his aim. How will it be for the future? Posterity will vainly ask for proof of his intellectual power, to invent, to organize, to administer. The historian must write that he aimed to increase the executive power, the central government, and to weaken the local power of the States; that he preferred the Federal authority to State rights, the judiciary to the legislature, the government to the people, the claims of money to the rights of man. Calhoun will stand as the representative of State rights and free trade; Clay, of the American system of protection; Benton, of payment in sound coin; some other, of the revenue tariff. And in the greatest question of the age, the question of Human Rights, as champions of mankind, there will appear Adams, Giddings, Chase, Palfrey, Mann, Hale, Rantoul, and Sumner; yes, one other name, which on the historian's page will shade all these, — the name of GARRISON. Men will recount the words of Webster at Plymouth Rock, at Bunker Hill, at Faneuil Hall, at Niblo's Garden; they will also recollect that he declared "protection of property" to be the great domestic object of government; that he said, "Liberty first and Union afterwards" was delusion and folly;" that he called on Massachusetts to conquer her "prejudices" in favor of unalienable right, and with alacrity give up a man to be a slave; turned all the North into a hunting-field for the blood-hound; that he made the negation of God the first principle of government; that our New England elephant turned round, tore Freedom's standard down, and trod her armies under foot. They will see that he did not settle the greatest questions by Justice and the Law of God. His parallel lines of power are indeed long lines, — a nation reads his word: they are not far apart, you cannot get many centuries between; for there are no great ideas of Right, no mighty acts of Love, to keep them wide.

There are brave words which Mr. Webster has spoken that will last while English is a speech; yea, will journey with the Anglo-Saxon race, and one day be classic in either hemisphere, in every zone. But what will posterity say of his efforts to chain the fugitive, to extend the area of human bondage; of his haughty scorn of any law higher than what trading politicians enact in the Capitol? "There is a law above all the enactments of human codes, the same throughout the world, the same in all time;" "it is the law written by the finger of God upon the heart of man; and by that law, unchangeable and eternal, while men despise fraud, and loathe rapine, and abhor blood, they will reject with indignation the wild and guilty fantasy that man can hold property in man." *

* Lord Brougham's speech on Negro Slavery, in the House of Commons, July 13, 1830.

Calhoun, Clay, Webster — they were all able men, — long in politics, all ambitious, grasping at the Presidency, all failing of what they sought. All three called themselves "Democrats," taking their stand on the unalienable rights of man. But all three conjoined to keep every sixth man in the nation a chattel slave; all three at last united in deadly war against the unalienable rights of men whom swarthy mothers bore. O democratic America!

Was Mr. Webster's private life good? There are many depraved things done without depravity of heart. I am here to chronicle, and not invent. I cannot praise a man for virtues that he did not have. This day, such praise sounds empty and impertinent as the chattering of a caged canary amid the sadness of a funeral prayer. Spite of womanly tenderness, it is not for me to renounce my manhood and my God. I shall

> "Naught extenuate and nothing add,
> Nor set down aught in malice."

Before he left New Hampshire, I find no stain upon his conduct there, save recklessness of expense. But in Boston, when he removed here, there were men in vogue worse than any since as conspicuous, — open debauchees. He fell in with them, and became over-fond of animal delights, of the joys of the body's baser parts; fond of sensual luxury, the victim of low appetites. He loved power, loved pleasure, loved wine. Let me turn off my face, and say no more of this sad theme: others were as bad as he.*

He was intensely proud. Careless of money, he was often in trouble on its account. He contracted debts, and did not settle; borrowed of rich and poor, and young and old, and rendered not again. Private money often clove

* Hoc sat viator: reliqua non sinit pudor;
Tu suspicare et ambula.

to his hands; yet in his nature there was no taint of avarice. He lavished money on luxuries, while his washerwoman was left unpaid; few Americans have spent so much as he. Rapacious to get, he was prodigal of his own. I wish the charges brought against his public administration may be disproved, whereof the stain rests on him to this day. When he entered on a lawyer's life, Mr. Gore advised him, "Whatever bread you eat, let it be the bread of independence!" Oh that the great mind could have kept that counsel! But, even at Portsmouth, luxury brought debt, and many an evil on its back. He collected money, and did not pay! "Bread of independence," when did he eat it last? Rich men paid his debts of money when he came to Massachusetts; they took a dead-pledge on the man; only death redeemed that mortgage. In 1827 he solicited the Senatorship of Massachusetts; it "would put down the calumnies of Isaac Hill"! He obtained the office, not without management. Then he refused to take his seat until ten thousand dollars was raised for him. The money came clandestinely, and he went into the Senate — a pensioner! His reputation demanded a speech against the tariff of '28; his pension required his vote for that "bill of abominations." He spoke one way, and voted the opposite. Was that the first *dotation?* He was forestalled before he left New Hampshire. The next gift was twenty thousand, it is said. Then the sums increased. What great "gifts" have been privately raised for him by contributions, subscriptions, donations, and the like! Is it honest to buy up a man? honest for a man to sell himself? Is it just for a judge who administers the law to take a secret bribe of a party at his court? Is it just for a party to offer such gifts? Answer Lord Bacon who tried it; answer Thomas More who tried it not. It is worse for a Maker of laws to be bought and sold. New England men, I hope not meaning wrong, bought the great senator in '27, and long held him in their pay. They gave him all his services were worth, — gave more. His commercial and financial policy has been the bane of New England and the North. In 1850 the South bought him, but never paid! *

A Senator of the United States, he was pensioned by the capitalists of Boston. Their "gifts" in his hand, how could he dare be just! His later speeches smell of bribes. Could not Francis Bacon warn him, nor either Adams guide? Three or four hundred years ago, Thomas More, when "under Sheriff of London," would not accept a pension from the king, lest it might swerve him from his duty to the town; when chancellor, he would not accept five thousand pounds which the English clergy publicly offered him, for public service done as chancellor. But Webster in private took — how much I cannot tell! Considering all things, his buyers' wealth and his unthriftiness, it was as dishonorable in them to bribe, as in him to take their gift!

To gain his point, alas! he sometimes treated facts, law, constitution, morality and religion, as an advocate treats matters at the bar. Was he certain South Carolina had no constitutional right to nullify? I make no doubt he felt so; but in his language he is just as strong when he declares the Fugitive Slave Bill is perfectly constitutional; that slavery cannot be in California and New Mexico; just as confident in his dreadful mock at conscience, and the dear God's unchanging law. He heeded not "the delegated voice of God" which speaks in the conscience of the faithful man.

No living man has done so much to debauch the conscience of the nation; to debauch the press, the pulpit, the forum, and the bar! There is no higher law, quoth he; and how much of the pulpit, the press, the forum, and the bar,

* "Sed lateri nullus comitem circumdare quærit,
Quem dat purus amor, sed quem tulit impia merces,
Nec quisquam vero pretium largitur amico,
Quem regat ex æquo, vicibusque regatur ab illo:
Sed miserum parva stipe munerat, ut pudibundos
Exercere sales inter *consilia* possit."

denies its God! Read the journals of the last week for proof of what I say; and read our history since March of '50. He poisoned the moral wells of society with his lower law, and men's consciences died of the murrain of beasts, which came because they drank thereat.

In an age which prizes money as the greatest good, and counts the understanding as the highest human faculty, the man who is to lead and bless the world must indeed be great in intellect, but also great in conscience, greater in affection, and greatest of all things in his soul. In his later years, Webster was intellect, and little more. If he did not regard the eternal Right, how could he guide a nation to what is useful for to-day? If he scorned the law of God, how could he bless the world of men? It was by this fault he fell. "Those who murdered Banquo, what did they win by it?"

——— "A barren sceptre in their gripe,
Thence to be wrenched with an unlineal hand,
No son of theirs succeeding."

He knew the cause of his defeat, and in the last weeks of his life confessed that he was deceived; that, before his fatal speech, he had assurance from the North and South, that, if he supported slavery, it would lead him into place and power; but now he saw the mistake, and that a few of the "fanatics" had more influence in America than he and all the South! He sinned against his own conscience, and so he fell!

He made him wings of slavery to gain a lofty eminence. Those wings unfeathered in his flight. For one and thirty months he fell, until at last he reached the tomb. There, on the sullen shore, a mighty wreck, great Webster lies.

"Is this the man in Freedom's cause approved,
The man so great, so honored, so beloved?
Where is the heartfelt worth and weight of soul,
Which labor could not stoop, nor fear control?

Where the known dignity, the stamp of awe,
Which, half abashed, the proud and venal saw?
Where the calm triumphs of an honest cause? —
Where the delightful taste of just applause?

Oh, lost alike to action and repose,
Unwept, unpitied in the worst of woes;
With all that conscious, undissembled pride,
Sold to the insults of a foe defied;
With all that habit of familiar fame,
Doomed to exhaust the dregs of life in shame!"

Oh, what a warning was his fall!

"To dash corruption in her proud career,
And teach her slaves that vice was born to fear."

"Oh dumb be passion's stormy rage,
When he who might
Have lighted up and led his age
Falls back in night."

Had he been faithful to his own best words, so oft repeated, how he would have stood! How different would have been the aspect of the North and the South; of the press, the pulpit, the forum, and the court!

Had he died after the treaty of 1842, how different would have been his fame!

Since the Revolution, no American has had so noble an opportunity as Mr. Webster to speak a word for the advancement of mankind. There was a great occasion: slavery was clamorous for new power, new territory; was invading the State Rights of the North. Earnest men in the North, getting aroused and hostile to slavery, were looking round for some able man to take the political guidance of the anti-slavery feeling, to check the great national crime, and help end it; they were asking —

"Who is the honest man, —
He that doth still and strongly good pursue,
To God, his neighbor, and himself, most true;
Whom neither fear nor fawning can
Unpin, or wrench from giving all their due?"

Some circumstances seemed to point to Mr. Webster as the man; his immense oratorical abilities, his long acquaintance with public affairs, his conspicuous position, his noble words in behalf of freedom, beginning with his college days and extending over many a year,—all these were powerful arguments in his behalf. The people had always been indulgent to his faults, allowing him a wide margin of public and private oscillation; the North was ready to sustain him in all generous efforts for the unalienable rights of man. But he threw away the great moment of his life, used all his abilities to destroy those rights of man, and builded the materials of honorable fame into a monument of infamy for the warning of mankind. Declaring that "the protection of property" was "the great object of government," he sought to unite the Money power of the North and the Slave power of the South into one great instrument to stifle discussion, and withstand religion, and the Higher Law of God.

Had he lived and labored for freedom as for slavery,—nay, with half the diligence and half the power,—to-morrow, all the North would rise to make him their President, and put on that Olympian brow the wreath of honor from a people's hand. Then he would have left a name like Adams, Jefferson, and Washington; and the tears of every good man would have dropped upon his tomb! Had he served his God with half the zeal that he served the South, He would not, in his age, have left him naked to his enemies! If Mr. Webster had cultivated the moral, the affectional, the religious part of his nature with half the diligence he nursed his power of speech, what a man there would have been! With his great ability as an advocate, with his eloquence, his magnetic power, in his position,—a Senator for twenty years,—if he could have attained the justice, the philanthropy, the religion of Channing or of Follen, or of many a modest woman in all the Christian sects, what a noble spectacle should we have seen! Then the nation would long since have made him President, and he also would have revolutionized men's ideas of political greatness; "the bigot would have ceased to persecute, the despot to vex, the desolate poor to suffer, the slave to groan and tremble, the ignorant to commit crimes, and the ill-contrived law to engender criminality."

But he did not fall all at once. No man ever does. Apostasy is not a sudden sin. Little by little he came to the ground. Long leaning, he leaned over and fell down. This was his great error — he sold himself to the money power to do service against mankind. The form of service became continually worse. Was he conscious of this corruption? — at first? But shall he bear the blame alone? Oh, no! Part of it belongs to this city, which corrupted him, tempted him with a price, bought him with its gold! Daniel Webster had not thrift. "Poor Richard" was no saint of his. He loved luxury, and was careless of wealth. Boston caught him by the purse; by that she led him to his mortal doom. With her much fair speech she caused him to yield; with the flattery of her lips she deceived him. Boston was the Delilah that allured him; but oft he broke the withes of gold, until at last, with a pension, she shore off the seven locks of his head, his strength went from him, and the Philistines took him and put out his eyes, brought him down to Washington, and bound him with fetters of brass. And he did grind in their prison-house; and they said, "Our God, which is slavery, hath delivered into our hands our enemy, the destroyer of our institutions, who slew many of us." Then, having used him for their need, they thrust the man away, deceived and broken-hearted!

No man can resist infinite temptation. There came a peril greater than he could bear. Condemn the sin — pity the offending man. The tone of political morality is pitiably low. It lowered him, and then he debased the morals of politics.

Part of the blame belongs to the New England church, which honors "devoutness," and sneers at every noble, manly life, calling men saints who only pray, all careless of the dead men's bones which glut the whited sepulchre. The churches of New England were waiting to proclaim slavery, and renounce the law of God. His is not all the blame. We must blame Mr. Webster as we blame few men. Society takes swift vengeance on the petty thief, the small swindler, and rogues in rags: the gallows kills the murderer. But for men in high office, with great abilities, who enact iniquity into law; who enslave thousands, and sow a continent with thraldom, to bear want and shame and misery and sin; who teach as political ethics the theory of crime, — for them there is often no earthly outward punishment, but the indignation with which mankind scourges the memory of the oppressor. From the judgment of men, the appeal lies to the judgment of God: He only knows who sins, and how much. How much Mr. Webster is to be pitied, we know right well. Had he been a clergyman, as once he wished, he might have passed through life with none of the outward blemishes which now deform his memory; famed for his gifts and graces too, for eloquence, and "soundness in the faith," "his praise in all the churches." Had he been a politician in a better age, — when it is not thought just for capitalists to buy up statesmen in secret, for politicians clandestinely to sell their services for private gold, or for clergymen, in the name of God, to sanctify all popular crimes, — he might have lifted up that noble voice continually for Truth and Right. Who could not in such a time? The straw blows with the wind. But, alas! he was not firm enough for his place; too weak in conscience to be the champion of justice while she needs a champion. Let us be just against the wrong he wrought, charitable to the man who wrought the wrong. Conscience compels our formidable blame; the affections weep their pity too.

Like Bacon, whom Mr. Webster resembles in many things, save industry and the philosophic mind, he had "no moral courage, no power of self-sacrifice or self-denial;" with strong passions, with love of luxury in all its forms, with much pride, great fondness of applause, and the intensest love of power; coming to Boston poor, a lawyer, without thrift, embarking in politics with such companions for his private and his public life, with such public opinion in the State, — that honesty is to serve the present purposes of your party, or the wealthy men who control it; in the Church, — that religion consists in belief without evidence, in ritual sacraments, in verbal prayer, — is it wonderful that this great intellect went astray? See how corrupt the churches are, — the leading clergy of America are the anointed defenders of man-stealing; see how corrupt is the State, betraying the red men, enslaving the black, pillaging Mexico; see how corrupt is trade, which rules the State and Church, dealing in men. Connecticut makes whips for the negro-driver. New Hampshire rears the negro-drivers themselves. Ships of Maine and Rhode Island are in the domestic slave-trade. The millionaires of Massachusetts own men in Virginia, Alabama, Missouri! The leading men in Trade, in Church and State, think justice is not much more needed in a statesman than it is needed in an ox, or in the steel which shoes his hoof! Remember these things, and pity Daniel Webster, ambitious, passionate, unthrifty; and see the circumstances which weighed him down. We judge the deeds: God only can judge the man. If you and I have not met the temptation which can overmaster us, let us have mercy on such as come bleeding from that battle.

His calling as a lawyer was somewhat dangerous, leading him "to make the worse appear the better reason;" to seek "not verity, but verisimilitude;" to look at the expedient end, not to inquire if his means be also just; to look too much at measures, not enough at principles. Yet his own brother

Ezekiel went safely through that peril, — no smell of that fire on his garment.

His intercourse with politicians was full of moral peril. How few touch politics, and are thenceforward clean!

Boston now mourns for him! She is too late in her weeping. She should have wept her warning when her capitalists filled his right hand with bribes. She ought to have put on sackcloth when the speech of March 7th first came here. She should have hung her flags at half-mast when the Fugitive Slave Bill became a law; then she only fired cannons, and thanked her representative. Webster fell prostrate, but was Boston more innocent than he? Remember the nine hundred and eighty-seven men that thanked him for the speech which touched their "conscience," and pointed out the path of "duty"! It was she that ruined him.

She bribed him in 1827, and often since. He regarded the sums thus paid as a retaining fee, and at the last maintained that the Boston manufacturers were still in his debt; for the services he had rendered them by defending the tariff in his place as Senator were worth more than all the money he received. Could a man be honest in such a position? Alas that the great orator had not the conscience to remember at first that man shall not live by bread alone!

What a sad life was his! His wife died, — a loving woman, beautiful, and tenderly beloved! Of several children, all save one have gone before him to the tomb. Sad man, he lived to build his children's monument! Do you remember the melancholy spectacle in the street, when Major Webster, a victim of the Mexican war, was by his father laid down in yonder tomb? — a daughter, too, but recently laid low! How poor seemed then the ghastly pageant in the street, empty and hollow as the muffled drum!

What a sad face he wore, — furrowed by passion, by ambition, that noble brow scarred all over with the records of a hard, sad life. Look at the prints and pictures of him in the street. I do not wonder his early friends abhor the sight. It is a face of sorrows, — private, public, secret woes. But there are pictures of that face in earlier years, full of power, but full of tenderness; the mouth feminine, and innocent as a girl's. What a life of passion, of dark sorrow, rolled betwixt the two! In that ambition-stricken face his mother would not have known her child!

For years to me, he has seemed like one of the tragic heroes of the Grecian tale, pursued by fate; and latterly, the saddest sight in all the Western World, — widowed of so much he loved, and grasping at what was not only vanity, but the saddest vexation of the heart. I have long mourned for him, as for no living or departed man. He blasted us with scornful lightning: him, if I could, I would not blast, but only bless continually and evermore.

You remember the last time he spoke in Boston; the procession, last summer, you remember it well. What a sad and care-worn countenance was that of the old man, welcomed with the mockery of applause! You remember, when the orator, wise-headed and friendly-hearted, came to thank him for his services, he said not a word of saving the Union; of the compromise measures, not a word. That farce was played out — it was only the tragic facts that were left; but for his great services he thanked him.

And when Webster replied, he said, "Here in Boston I am not disowned; at least, here I am not disowned." No, Daniel Webster, you are not disowned in Boston. So long as I have a tongue to teach, a heart to feel, you shall never be disowned. I must be just. I must be tender too!

It was partly by Boston's sin that the great man fell! I pity his victims; you pity them, too. But I pity him more, oh, far more! Pity the oppressed, will you? Will you not also pity the oppressor in his sin? Look there! See that face, so manly strong, so maiden meek! Hear that voice! "Neither do I condemn thee! Go, and sin no more!" Listen to the last words of the Crucified: "Father, forgive them; for they know not what they do."

The last time he was in Faneuil Hall, — it was "Faneuil Hall open;" once it had been shut — it was last May — the sick old man — you remember the feeble look and the sad face, the tremulous voice. He came to solicit the vote of the Methodists, a vain errand. I felt then that it was his last time, and forbore to look upon that saddened countenance.

The last time he was in the Senate, it was to hear his successor speak. He stayed an hour, and heard Charles Sumner demonstrate that the Fugitive Slave Bill was not good religion, nor good Constitution, nor good law. The old and the new stood face to face, — the Fugitive Slave Bill and Justice. What an hour! What a sight! What thoughts ran through the great man's mind, mingled with what regrets! For slavery never set well on him. It was a Nessus' shirt on our Hercules, and the poison of his own arrows rankled now in his own bones. Had Mr. Webster been true to his history, true to his heart, true to his intention and his promises, he would himself have occupied that ground two years before. Then there would have been no Fugitive Slave Bill, no chain round the court-house, no man-stealing in Boston; but the "Defender of the Constitution," become the "Defender of the unalienable rights of man," would have been the President of the United States! But he had not the courage to deliver the speech he made; no man can serve two masters, — Justice and Ambition. The mill of God grinds slow but dreadful fine!

He came home to Boston, and went down to Marshfield to die. An old man, broken with the storms of State, went home — to die! His neighbors came to ease the fall, to look upon the disappointment, and give him what cheer they could. To him, to die was gain; life was the only loss. Yet he did not wish to die: he surrendered, — he did not yield.

At the last end, his friends were about him; his dear ones — his wife, his son (the last of six children he had loved). Name by name he bade them all farewell, and all his friends, man by man. Two colored servants of his were there, — whom he had helped purchase out of slavery, and bless with freedom's life. They watched over the bedside of the dying man. The kindly doctor sought to sweeten the bitterness of death with medicated skill; and, when that failed, he gave the great man a little manna which fell down from heaven three thousand years ago, and shepherd David gathered up and kept it in a psalm: "The Lord is my Shepherd: though I walk through the valley of the shadow of death, I will fear no evil; thy rod and thy staff they comfort me."

And the great man faltered out his last words, "That is what I want — thy rod, thy rod; thy staff, thy staff." That heart had never wholly renounced its God. Oh, no! it had scoffed at His "higher law;" but, in the heart of hearts, there was religious feeling still!

Just four years after his great speech, on the 24th of October, all that was mortal of Daniel Webster went down to the dust, and the soul to the motherly bosom of God! Men mourn for him: he heeds it not. The great man has gone where the servant is free from his master, where the weary are at rest, where the wicked cease from troubling.

> "No further seek his merits to disclose,
> Or draw his frailties from their dread abode;
> There they alike in trembling hope repose,
> The bosom of his Father and his God!"

Massachusetts has lost her great adopted son. Has lost? Oh, no! "I still live" is truer than the sick man knew: —

> "He lives and spreads aloft by those pure eyes
> And perfect witness of all-judging God."

His memory will long live with us, still dear to many a loving heart. What honor shall we pay? Let the State go out mindful of his noblest services, yet tearful for his fall; sad that he would fain have filled him with the husks the swine do eat, and no man gave to him. Sad and tearful, let her remember the force of circumstances, and dark temptation's secret power. Let her remember that while we know what he yielded to, and what is sin, God knows what also is resisted, and HE alone knows who the sinner is. Massachusetts, the dear old mother of us all! Oh! let her warn her children to fling away ambition, and let her charge them, every one, that there is a God who must indeed be worshipped, and a higher law of God which must be kept, though Gold and Union fail. Then let her say to them, "Ye have dwelt long enough in this mountain; turn ye, and take your journey into the land of FREEDOM, which the Lord your God giveth you!"

Then let her lift her eyes to Heaven, and pray:—

"Sweet Mercy! to the gates of heaven
This statesman lead, his sins forgiven;
The rueful conflict, the heart riven
With vain endeavor,
And memory of earth's bitter leaven,
Effaced for ever!

But

—— why to him confine the prayer,
While kindred thoughts and yearnings bear,
On the frail heart, the purest share
With all that live?
The best of what we do and are,
Great God, forgive!"

www.ingramcontent.com/pod-product-compliance
Lightning Source LLC
LaVergne TN
LVHW021424110826
845150LV00007B/2079

* 9 7 8 1 4 2 5 5 0 7 6 0 2 *